Code-Mixin
A Hong K

D0682432

Multilingual Matters

"Bilingualism: Basic Principles" (Second edition)
HUGO BAETENS BEARDSMORE
"Evaluating Bilingual Education: A Canadian Case Study"
MERRILL SWAIN AND SHARON LAPKIN
"Bilingual Children: Guidance for the Family"
GEORGE SAUNDERS
"Language Attitudes Among Arabic-French Bilinguals in Morocco"
ABDELÂLI BENTAHILA
"Conflict and Language Planning in Quebec"
RICHARD Y. BOURHIS (ed.)
"Bilingualism and Special Education"
JIM CUMMINS
"Bilingualism or Not: The Education of Minorities"
TOVE SKUTNABB-KANGAS
"An Ethnographic/Sociolinguistic Approach to Language Proficiency Assessment"
CHARLENE RIVERA (ed.)
"Communicative Competence Approaches to Language Proficiency Assessment: Research and Application"
CHARLENE RIVERA (ed.)
"Language Proficiency and Academic Achievement"
CHARLENE RIVERA (ed.)
"Pluralism: Cultural Maintenance and Evolution"
BRIAN BULLIVANT
"Placement Procedures in Bilingual Education: Education and Policy Issues"
CHARLENE RIVERA (ed.)
"The Education of Linguistic and Cultural Minorities in the OECD Countries"
STACY CHURCHILL
"Learner Language and Language Learning"
CLAUS FAERCH, KIRSTEN HAASTRUP AND ROBERT PHILLIPSON
"Bilingual and Multicultural Education: Canadian Perspectives"
STAN SHAPSON AND VINCENT D'OYLEY (eds.)
"Multiculturalism: The Changing Australian Paradigm"
LOIS FOSTER AND DAVID STOCKLEY
"Language Acquisition of a Bilingual Child"
ALVINO FANTINI
"Modelling and Assessing Second Language Acquisition"
KENNETH HYLTENSTAM AND MANFRED PIENEMANN (eds.)
"Aspects of Bilingualism in Wales"
COLIN BAKER
"Minority Education and Ethnic Survival"
MICHAEL BYRAM
"Age in Second Language Acquisition"
BIRGIT HARLEY
"Language in a Black Community
VIV EDWARDS
"Language and Education in Multilingual Settings"
BERNARD SPOLSKY (ed.)
"The Interdisciplinary Study of Urban Bilingualism in Brussels"
ELS WITTE and HUGO BAETENS BEARDSMORE
"Introspection in Second Language Research"
CLAUS FAERCH and GABRIELE KASPER (eds.)

Please contact us for the latest information on all books in the series.

Derrick Sharp, General Editor, Multilingual Matters,
Bank House, 8a Hill Road, Clevedon, Avon BS21 7HH, England.

MULTILINGUAL MATTERS 27

Code-Mixing and Code Choice
A Hong Kong Case Study

John Gibbons

MULTILINGUAL MATTERS LTD
Clevedon · Philadelphia

To Mark and Ben

Library of Congress Catalog Number: 86-63640

British Library Cataloguing in Publication Data

Gibbons, John, 1946–
 Code-mixing and code choice: a Hong Kong
 case study.—(Multilingual matters; 27)
 1. Sociolinguistics—Hong Kong
 2. Hong Kong—Languages
 I. Title II. Series
 409'.51'25   P40.45.H85

 ISBN 0–905028–66–X
 ISBN 0–905028–65–1 pbk

Multilingual Matters Ltd,
Bank House, 8a Hill Road,
Clevedon, Avon BS21 7HH,
England.

Typeset by Photo·Graphics, Honiton, Devon
Printed and bound in Great Britain by
The Bath Press, Bath BA2 3BL.

Contents

Preface: Sociolinguistics and Hong Kong

Sociolinguistics as an area of study has experienced explosive growth over the past twenty years, with the appearance of many journals and books. Of interest in its own right, Sociolinguistics can also supply valuable information and ideas to linguists, sociologists, anthropologists and educationalists. After a period of varied approaches and disparate findings, discernible attempts are being made to evaluate, rationalize and integrate work in the field (see for example, Hudson, 1980; Dittmar, 1976; and Saville-Troike, 1982). In line with this trend, a major aim of this book is to use a range of different sociolinguistic approaches on a single speech community, in order both to test their analytical and descriptive value and to work towards a more unified descriptive framework. The focus is on language use rather than language proficiency (although the two are obviously related).

A colony in an era when such forms of government have been widely rejected and replaced, the position of Hong Kong as a Western outpost in the heart of Asia has resulted in a cultural cross-roads, a melting pot of Eastern and Western influences. A bustling economic success, Hong Kong was forced by massive immigration from China to use to the full the remarkable ingenuity, adaptability and grit of its people to provide the necessities of life. Partly as a consequence of the above, Hong Kong is of considerable linguistic interest. There are language communities from various regions of China, the sub-continent, and the West, as well as creole speakers from Macao (Thompson, 1960). Official language policy is one of Chinese–English bilingualism, in which the two languages co-exist uneasily. In spite of Hong Kong's potential interest, there has been relatively little research into the linguistic and sociolinguistic situation. Another aim of this study is to make a small contribution towards the stock of information available on language, particularly on code-mixing and code choice in Hong Kong. To keep the study within manageable bounds, the accessible, fairly homogeneous, bilingual community of students at the University of Hong Kong was used, since this is one of the few groups in

Hong Kong where one can rely (in most cases) on a reasonable bilingual proficiency, a pre-requisite for study of code choice.

The principal objectives of this work can therefore be summarized as follows:

1. to use and evaluate a number of sociolinguistic models and methods
2. to arrive at a more coherent model of code choice
3. to provide a substantial amount of information concerning the sociolinguistic behaviour of a specific Hong Kong group.

Acknowledgements

First and above all, I should like to thank all the students at the University of Hong Kong, who gave their time and their voices.

Grateful thanks are due for permission to print (in revised form) material which originally appeared elsewhere: *Anthropological Linguistics*, for part of Chapter 3, originally published as J. P. Gibbons, Code-mixing and Koinéising in the Speech of Students at the University of Hong Kong, *Anthropological Linguistics*, 21, 3, 1979, 113–23; *Journal of Multilingual and Multicultural Development*, for Chapter 6 originally published as J. Gibbons, Attitudes towards Languages and Code-Mixing in Hong Kong, *JMMD*, 4, 2 & 3, 1983, 129–47.

My gratitude also goes to:

in particular – Professors Frank Palmer and Peter Trudgill.
Informants and advisers on student speech behaviour – Chan Man Sing, Ng Mau Sang and Yip Koon Hung;
the staff of the Centre for Applied Statistics, University of Reading
the many friends and colleagues who helped, including John Bacon-Shone, Peter Barnes, Kingsley Bolton, Michael Bond, Paula Fleming, Howard Giles, Patrick Griffin, R. K. Johnson, Ora Kwo, Irina Lau, Leung Chung Sum, Christen deLinde, Carol Scotton, Peter Tung and Jeannie Wong;
and to my wife Pauline for patience and proof-reading.

1 The Language Situation in Hong Kong

Introduction

A broad understanding of the language situation in Hong Kong provides an essential context for the study of the speech behaviour of students at the University of Hong Kong, which acts in turn as a sounding board for the theoretical approaches discussed through this book. A good starting point for a general impression of Hong Kong's languages can be found in the government censuses of 1971 and 1981. Certain facts about the Hong Kong situation emerge in a striking fashion. First, despite Hong Kong's cosmopolitan multiracial appearance, in 1981 98% of the population was *Chinese* which means that Hong Kong is a far more racially homogeneous city than most in Britain and other western countries. This overwhelming numerical dominance of the Chinese population must affect the roles of languages in Hong Kong. A second salient fact is that Hong Kong is largely a first or second generation *migrant* community. For instance, in the period 1951–1981 there were more than a million immigrants into a population of around 5½ million. Third, the Hong Kong population is a *young* one. In 1981 the census figures were:

Under 15	: 24.8%
15–34	: 40.7%
35–64	: 27.9%
65 and over	: 6.6%
	100%

The information about language from the 1981 census had not been released when this was written. In the 1971 census we find that Cantonese is the "usual language" of 88% of the population. Speakers of other Chinese dialects form 10.29% of the population while English is the "usual

1

language" of only 1.04%. On this measure English falls below some comparatively obscure Chinese dialects.

A different picture emerges when we turn to the "ability to speak English" of non-native speakers. Some 25% of the population claim to speak English — 30% of men compared to 20% of women. This ability may, of course, be only marginal.

Unfortunately the census statistics provide little more information on language in Hong Kong. Consequently, some of the information in the rest of this chapter cannot be related to data and is therefore impressionistic, although reference to published information is made wherever possible.

Languages in Hong Kong

Cantonese

Cantonese is normally classified as a Chinese "dialect". According to Fraenkel (1967: 76) it has some 55 million speakers — a significant number. Mandarin and Cantonese are not mutually intelligible (although it is possible for their speakers to develop an understanding of the other's speech — see below).

The Cantonese of Hong Kong is fairly close to the Guangzhou (Canton) norm, reflecting mutual influence and the fact that many of Hong Kong's people have their origins in the region around Guangzhou. Some phonological changes appear to be in progress, however (Pan, 1982). There is no standard reference work for Cantonese but useful information can be found in Cheung (1972) and Hashimoto (1972).

Mandarin

Hereafter the chief spoken form of Chinese, also known as *Putonghua* and *Kow yü*, will be referred to by its best known English name — Mandarin. Useful linguistic descriptions can be found in Kratochvíl (1970) and Chao (1968). Mandarin is the national standard language (in slightly different forms) of Hong Kong's giant neighbour the People's Republic of China, and of Taiwan, and is an official language in Singapore. It is said to have in excess of 600 million speakers, the largest number of speakers of any language in the world, although the degree and type of proficiency of these speakers remain unverified. It is being adopted as a *lingua franca* among overseas Chinese communities.

In these circumstances one might expect Mandarin to play an important role as a second spoken language in Hong Kong. In fact this is not the case. It is taught to children in only a very small number of schools. For most Chinese people in Hong Kong, their major contact with Mandarin is through entertainment. The most common form is cinema, but it can also include popular songs and television programmes. In consequence many Hong Kong Chinese have some degree of listening comprehension ability in Mandarin, but are able to speak the language poorly, if at all. The listening ability is fostered by sub-titles and by regular phonological correspondences between Cantonese and Mandarin. The forthcoming changes in Hong Kong's political status will presumably lead to much more widespread attempts to learn Mandarin in Hong Kong.

Other Chinese Dialects

We have already noted that most of Hong Kong's population consists of immigrants or the descendants of immigrants: at the time of the British takeover the population could be numbered in thousands. Although most Hong Kong people trace their origins to Cantonese speaking areas, a sizeable minority originate from areas where other Chinese dialects are spoken. This minority brought their mother tongue with them, but now appear to be following a classic integrative pattern, by adopting the dominant local language — Cantonese (Fishman & Hofman, 1966, give an account of this same process in the U.S.A.). The 1971 census statistics show this clearly (see Table 1).

TABLE 1

| Age Group | Usual Language | | |
	Cantonese	Other Chinese Dialects	Others
14 and below	92.1%	6.7%	1.2%
15 – 24	91.8%	6.9%	1.3%
25 – 39	87.2%	9.9%	2.9%
40 – 54	83.4%	15.3%	1.3%
55 and over	78.8%	20.5%	0.7%

One consequence is that schooling in dialects other than Cantonese has now virtually disappeared in Hong Kong. If these dialects are maintained, their use is limited largely to the home, and to certain small enclaves.

Written Chinese

A major unifying force among China's linguistically disparate peoples is their written system which, because it is fundamentally ideographic rather than phonetic (i.e. characters tend to represent meanings more than sounds), is capable of transcribing a large number of related languages/ dialects (and, with modifications, unrelated or distantly related languages such as Japanese and Vietnamese) — see Newnham (1971) for details. The Chinese written language is of great antiquity, and over time written Chinese and the various spoken languages of China have diverged, although an attempt is now being made in mainland China to bring the written language nearer to the spoken. Since the government of China has resided in the north for a long period, the written language has been in a dynamic relationship of mutual influence with Mandarin — the spoken language of government and the capital. The result of the historical divergence, in conjunction with the influence of spoken Mandarin, is that written Chinese is different in many respects from Cantonese: differences include vocabulary, grammar and forms of expression. Consequently for Cantonese children learning written Chinese has some of the properties of learning a second language.

The accepted standard for written Chinese in Hong Kong is essentially traditional and literary (see Hsü, 1979: 130ff). The simplified characters and more colloquial style of mainland written Chinese are less usual in Hong Kong, and are found largely in publications with some specific allegiance to the People's Republic of China. There is also considerable variation in Hong Kong written Chinese, running from full literary Chinese to the equivalent of Cantonese written in characters. Educated Chinese immediately recognize the latter as deviant, and tend to be highly critical of the popular press in which it occurs.

English

As noted previously English is the usual language of only one per cent of people in Hong Kong, although approximately a quarter of the population claim some proficiency. As one would expect, given Hong Kong's colonial status the official norm is British English. Nevertheless, American English is not uncommon, partly because more Hong Kong people receive University education in North America than in Britain or Hong Kong. The English spoken by Chinese in Hong Kong runs along a continuum. from heavily Cantonese influenced variants to standard British English. Hunter (1974) points out that there is no local norm, unlike the second language situation in India, Singapore or Kenya. However, Luke & Richards (1982) document "certain recognizable and distinctive features" of the middle proficiency Hong Kong English speaker.

Pidgin English

Whinnom (1971: 104) writes, concerning the "modern situation" in Hong Kong:

> "Pidgin is the language of Chinese. . . . It is the language in which the amah from Canton communicates with the cook-boy from Shanghai, and in which the shopkeeper will address a fellow trader from Fuchow."

In the article Whinnom makes a case for pidgin English being a *lingua franca* (everyday language of communication among speakers of different mother tongues) in certain Chinese social groups. In personal communication Whinnom has remarked that this situation existed during his period of residence in Hong Kong in the 1950's. However, one can say with some confidence that, apart from the occasional relic speaker, pidgin English has virtually disappeared in Hong Kong. The best available description of China coast pidgin English is Hall (1944).

Roles of Languages in Hong Kong

From what has been said so far it is apparent that the languages mainly used in Hong Kong are (spoken) Cantonese, Written Chinese and English. What follows is a brief summary of the roles played by these languages in various domains of Hong Kong life – more detailed descriptions can be found in Gibbons (1983) and Luke & Richards (1982). In keeping with normal Hong Kong practice when the term "Chinese" is used in this book it should be taken to mean spoken Cantonese and Written Chinese.

The Media

In newspapers, radio and television there is more Chinese than English, although English appears over-represented given the number of speakers.

Law and Government

There is official parity of English and Chinese, although in practice English appears to have precedence in authority, and Chinese in frequency of use. The internal written language of law and the Civil Service is English.

Business and Employment

Cantonese (occasionally with additive material from English) is the normal spoken language of the Chinese business community. Because of its prestige connotations and suitability to the appurtenances of the modern office (typewriters, computers etc.) English is comparatively common in writing, especially in the higher echelons. Hong Kong people place great importance on the learning of English for employment purposes, in part because they are well aware that a knowledge of English correlates with income, prestige of employment and educational level (Westcott, 1977).

Education

There is a 2% minority (Education Department figures) of expatriate children who attend schools with German, French, Japanese, American, British and other curricula. The remaining (mostly Chinese) 98% of children attend schools where the curriculum relates to Hong Kong and the language of instruction ("medium") is officially either English or Chinese. The situation regarding the medium of instruction in such schools, expressed in terms of percentages of students enrolled in March 1980, was the following:

Primary schools: Chinese medium: 91.4%; English medium: 8.6%
Secondary schools: Chinese medium: 12.3%; English medium: 87.7%

(Education Department figures). The change of medium between primary and secondary schools is startling and has been the cause of much public controversy, although it has been brought about mainly by parental demand. In reality the situation is not so clear cut, since both languages are used in most schools whatever the ostensible medium. For a more detailed discussion of this issue see Gibbons (1982).

At the tertiary level the University of Hong Kong is primarily English medium although Cantonese is used in tutorials on occasions. The Chinese University is predominantly Chinese medium (i.e. Written Chinese and spoken Cantonese); however, English (particularly reading matter) and

Mandarin speech are also used. In the two Polytechnics most writing is in English but Cantonese is not uncommon in spoken instruction. Of the three teacher training colleges, two are officially entirely English medium and the third offers courses taught in both English and Chinese. The other three "recognized" tertiary colleges have a mixture of language media. Overall at the tertiary level there is a strong tendency for reading material to be in English while speech is in Cantonese whatever the official language policy of the institution concerned.

Status of English and Chinese

The *lingua francas* of Hong Kong mirror a social division between Westerners and Chinese. Despite the significant numbers of French and German speakers, the *lingua franca* of Westerners in Hong Kong is English. For instance, a small scale survey of children from German speaking homes showed that nearly all of those who had been in Hong Kong for more than a year had a high level of proficiency in English. Among Chinese, however, the *lingua franca* is Cantonese (and written Chinese). The language shift to Cantonese among speakers of other Chinese languages has already been documented. Luke & Richards (1982) believe that this is a result of a high degree of "enclosure", that is that Chinese and expatriates essentially live in isolated communities: they refer (p. 52) to "separate life styles and value systems and . . . little interaction between the two groups". In this respect Hong Kong may not be markedly different from other societies with substantial transient expatriate communities. Luke & Richards (1982: 58) also point out that frequent Cantonese–English code-switching "is not a common feature of the speech repertoire of Hong Kong Cantonese".

The status of English in Hong Kong is somewhat unusual. In countries such as India, Ivory Coast or Mozambique the former colonial language is a *lingua franca* of the educated local élite, comprising one common form of local *internal* communication — these might be seen as true *second language* situations. As far as the local Hong Kong population is concerned, English does not play such a role: its uses in internal communication are predominantly limited to official writing — Chinese rarely speak English to one another. By contrast in Chile or Poland, Spanish and Polish respectively serve for all purposes of internal communication — other languages are learnt essentially for *external* communication. These comprise true *foreign language* situations. Since English in Hong Kong is used in both education and the law, it cannot be said to be a foreign language in this sense. In consequence Luke & Richards (1982) refer to the status of English in Hong Kong as an "auxiliary language".

Language Attitudes

Language attitudes frequently reflect the history and current position of different linguistic groups within a society (see, for example, Edwards, 1979). Fu (1979) gives a lucid historical survey of language in education in Hong Kong. She shows how colonial governments frequently accorded an inferior role to the Chinese language. It is only in the post-war era that Chinese has come to be treated as a partner with English. Chinese attitudes to the West were similar. The Chinese view of themselves as superior and of outsiders as barbarians is well documented (see for example Wright, 1953). These historical legacies are likely to influence attitudes to English and Chinese.

In the current situation there are a number of factors which may influence attitudes. The first is that English native speakers in Hong Kong mostly comprise an élite group. They tend to be skilled professionals with good incomes. Relations between Chinese and Westerners generally appear to lack antagonism, but are not particularly warm. Turning to the Chinese population, one should remember that proficiency in English correlates with educational level, prestigious employment, and (not least) with income.

Another possible influence on language attitudes is the spread of the international (but English language) 'pop' culture, especially among younger people in Hong Kong. For instance, some Cantonese radio stations play a significant proportion of English language records. Local fashion and film magazines refer often to the West, and incorporate fragments of English. Chinese traditional dress, hair styles and entertainment tend to be replaced by Western imports, or local hybrids of East and West. Indeed, to some extent, the same could be said of architecture, arts, government and education, and even (to a lesser degree) of eating habits. Nevertheless most Chinese people in Hong Kong appear to have a strong sense of Chineseness and to be proud of their national identity.

The study of language attitudes in this setting is of evident interest. In fact this may be the best studied area in language research in Hong Kong. There have been a number of attitude studies, nearly all using Chinese students in secondary schools or universities, examining attitudes towards English and Chinese. This is useful for the purposes of this book, although the results of these studies obviously cannot be taken as necessarily representing the attitudes of the wider community.

The first published study to examine attitudes in depth was Cheng, Shek, Tse & Wong (1973). Their work is unashamedly polemical, and the first sentence reads: "This is not a piece of 'academic' research". It revealed a strong emotional attachment to Chinese allied to an unemotional and pragmatic acceptance of English as important to self-advancement and a good career. They found little hostility towards English.

Fu (1975) administered a controlled questionnaire to 561 secondary school students. Fu (1975: 174) summarizes the findings as follows:

"Predictably, students see (1) English as an important and necessary subject, but (2) they do not feel easy about using it in speech. (3) They take pride in their own Chinese civilization, but (4) have generally negative attitudes toward western civilization and towards English speaking people."

One can see that, while attitudes to Chinese are fairly clear cut, attitudes towards English are both negative and positive — Fu uses the term "ambivalent". This ambivalence towards English finds a complex psychological explanation in "boomerang" and "fore-warning" effects in the experimental studies of Yang & Bond (1980) and Bond & Yang (1982).

Lyczak, Fu & Ho (1976) undertook a matched guise study of attitudes to English and Chinese speakers. They played tapes of bilingual speakers using both English and Chinese, for judgement of the speakers by students (further details of the matched guise technique are available in Chapter 6). They found that:

"Chinese guises were rated significantly more kind, trustworthy, honest, considerate, serious of purpose, humble and friendly. English guises were rated sigificantly more good looking, intelligent, well-off and competent." (Lyczak, Fu & Ho, 1976: 430)

A principal components analysis with rotation (see Lyczak *et al.*, 1976) revealed two factors. The first, consisting of "friendly, trustworthy, honest, kind, humble and considerate", appears to be a reaction of positive affect, of solidarity, and characterizes the Chinese speakers. The second appears to be a status or prestige factor, consisting of "intelligent, competent, industrious, (high) status of occupation, serious of purpose, well-off and good looking": this factor characterized the English speakers.

Despite the ambivalence it is interesting to note how well Hong Kong language attitudes accord with Ryan's (1979: 155) description:

"The fundamental distinction developed in this chapter contrasts *status* or *prestige*, the value of a speech variety for social advancement, and *solidarity*, the value of a variety for identification with a group." (My emphasis.)

Ryan points out that this distinction is found in many studies performed in disparate societies. The Chinese population of Hong Kong is no exception with English attracting "prestige" connotations and Cantonese "solidarity" connotations. More evidence for this is presented in Chapter 6.

2 The Sociology of Language Approach

Introduction

Sociolinguistics as a field concerns itself with the complex yet systematic relations between social factors and choices both between languages and within a language (hereafter both of the latter are referred to as "code choice"). The range and complexity of the issues involved have given rise to a number of different approaches which occasionally take on the properties of specific "schools" (for instance, "ethnography of speaking", see Bauman & Sherzer, 1974). These approaches are rarely discrete — indeed mutual influence is the rule rather than the exception. Trudgill (1978: 1–18) provides a lucid theoretical overview of the various approaches. This book does not cover the same ground but rather attempts to evaluate the approaches *in use* on a single community of speakers. A brief description of the approach begins each chapter, in most cases discussing the theoretical orientation, the method of data collection and the model for analysis and presentation of the findings. This is followed by a description of a study of Hong Kong student speech in which the approach was utilized, and the chapter normally ends with an evaluation of the approach based in part on the experience of applying it.

The first requirement of an investigation into a specific speech community is a broad general picture of that community's language behaviour. This is of value in itself and also provides a context for more detailed studies. As Pride & Holmes (1972: 7) write:

"The study of social meaning conveyed by different languages in a multilingual community can be undertaken at two levels, the one logically preceding the other. In the first place one can examine the way languages are used on the macro-scale, using large-scale surveys to reveal community norms of language use. Then against this background one can examine how the individual exploits his awareness of the society's norms in order to achieve particular effects."

In view of this the first sociolinguistic approach that was used was the Sociology of Language approach commonly associated with Fishman. This attempts to correlate physical and social context with choices between different languages. Fishman (1971b: 583) describes it as follows:

> "habitual language choice in multilingual speech communities or speech networks is far from being a random matter of momentary inclination, even under those circumstances when it could very well function as such from a purely probabilistic point of view (Lieberson, 1964). 'Proper' usage dictates that only *one* of the theoretically co-available languages or varieties *will* be chosen by particular classes of *interlocutors* on particular kinds of *occasions* to discuss particular kinds of *topics*."

In Fishman's familiar terms we are asking *who* speaks *what language* to *whom*, *where* and *when*. This kind of code choice is sometimes referred to as "situational code-switching".

Much of the early work in the "ethnography of speaking" shared similar aims and approaches. In particular Hymes (1977) details many varied elements of context which have been shown to influence language choices. Fishman, Cooper & Ma *et al.* (1971) also show how various contextual elements may be grouped into "social domains". The actual framework used here derives from the clear and comprehensive one given in Ervin-Tripp (1964). The relevant elements of Ervin-Tripp's framework can be summarized as follows:

SETTING
   – locale: time, place
   – situation (what is happening)
   – style
PARTICIPANTS
   – status: sex, age, occupation
   – role
TOPIC

A number of key concepts have been developed by scholars working this area and some are used here. They include *code* — a neutral term used to refer both to a language and to a variety of a language, and *speech community* which is transparent in that it refers to a group that shares a code, but is also somewhat tendentious — see Saville–Troike (1982: especially Chapters 2 and 3) and Hudson (1980: 25–30).

Method

Within Sociology of Language studies there are two principal ways of gaining information about code choice in relation to contextual factors. One can ask speakers what they do, or one can observe their behaviour: in other words census techniques or ethnographic study. The latter method is discussed and applied in Chapter 4.

The census questionnaire approach has the great advantage of being well suited to very large scale studies, being comparatively simple and cheap to administer. It also permits the gathering of specific and directly comparable data from a large number of subjects — something that can cause great problems in observational studies. Its limitations relate to the accuracy one can expect in responses. First, subjects may be unaware of certain aspects of their language behaviour. Second, they may view their own language behaviour with a prejudiced eye. Essentially, census and questionnaire studies ask people what they *think* they do, rather than probing their actual behaviour. As Lieberson (1969: 286) remarks:

"There are aspects of bilingualism for which the [census] instrument is inadequate. If a population were surveyed about their diglossia, for example, there is reason to believe that many would be unaware of, or would at least deny, their use of the low variety."

Examples of questionnaire studies can be found in Fishman, Cooper & Ma *et al.* (1971), Barcelona (1977), Whiteley (1974): see also Ohanessian, Ferguson & Polomé (1975).

Model

Many researchers within this area present their findings as a hierarchically ordered series of decisions, leading to code choices. Figures 1 and 2 are examples from Rubin (1968) based on questionnaire data, and from Sankoff (1972) based on observation.

Such a model can also be recast as a flow-chart algorithm (see Ervin-Tripp, 1969: 93 ff). The advantages of this model are apparent. It can present with great economy the decision making process underlying code choice. However, most studies of human behaviour show probabilistic patterning rather than simple decisions, and the same may hold true of code choice. Hence Fishman, Cooper & Ma *et al.* (1971) present their findings in terms of statistical probabilities. This does not mean that this type of decision tree is not usable, but rather that it operates with two qualifications. First (as users intend), it should be seen as displaying social norms

FIGURE 1   *Ordered dimensions in the choice of language*

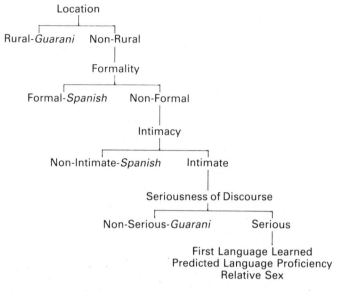

Source: Rubin, 1968: 109

(which can be violated) rather than absolute decisions. Second, it forms only part of a complete model, that part which handles certain code choices which can be simply explained by certain contexts: other choices may need to be described in more overtly probabilistic terms.

Applying the Sociology of Language Approach

Data Collection

The Instrument

To discover the relationship between code choice and the factors mentioned above, researchers have in the past used questionnaire techniques, which in essence ask informants "what language do you speak to *z* type person in *y* situation to discuss topic *x*". As stated previously there are two major problems associated with this approach. The first is that the informants may not always be conscious of the totality of their language behaviour; the second is that language can be (and in Hong Kong almost certainly is) an intensely emotional issue, with the consequent possibility of distortion of the informants' view of their own language behaviour.

FIGURE 2 *Factors constraining code choice for the Buang*

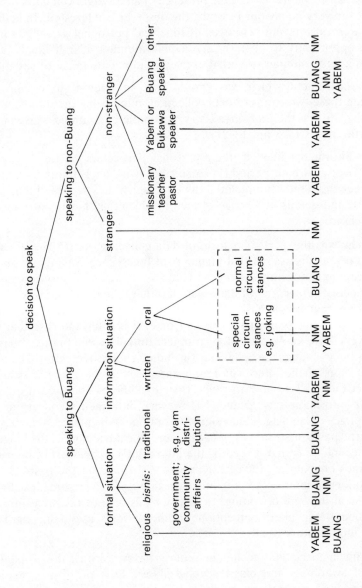

(NM = Neo-Melanesian, - - - indicates optional distinction.)
Source: Sankoff, 1972: 39

The other type of data collection most commonly used is observation. However, this method also has its problems — principally the Observer's Paradox (see Chapter 4) that the presence of an observer can influence and distort the very behaviour in which the observer is interested. In addition there were insufficient resources of time and personnel as well as insufficient opportunity to observe an adequate number of individuals taking part in a large number of verbal exchanges in a wide range of situations.

The instrument which was chosen was an attempt to compromise between these two forms of data collection, minimizing the disadvantages of both. This was the *Language Diary*. A completed example is given in the following pages (see pp. 18–21).

The informants filled in their personal particulars on the first page. Then, over a 24 hour period (in some cases work days, in others holidays and weekends) they completed a table on which they recorded their code choices, and details of a range of factors which may have contributed to these choices.

Why was this particular form of data collection used? The objective was to reveal any system that members of this speech community may be operating in choosing their codes. To do so, it was necessary to examine the students' *perceptions* of the situation rather than the realities, since it is the former that are the basis of the students' decisions. To give an example, when two strangers meet for the first time, it is often the case that they have very little knowledge of each other. Initially assumptions about the appropriacy of language behaviour (including choice of code) will be made on the basis of the interlocutor's appearance and role. As the strangers interact they will be able to refine their hypotheses about each other as further information is gleaned. However, judgements concerning the appropriacy of language behaviour will continue to be made on the basis of the participants' assessments of each other. One advantage of the language diary technique is that it records the informant's *judgements* of interlocutors, thus enabling us to see how speakers behave on the basis of their perceptions of interlocutors; in other words we are given some insight into the system they are operating. In fact, for this type of research, information about the speaker's perceptions of others is more useful than hard data about interlocutors.

The language diary technique reduces in several ways the problems of lack of awareness and bias discussed above. First the task is made as objective and concrete as possible, by requiring the recording of well-defined factors in columns. This also avoids problems caused by a lack of awareness of the totality of crucial factors since the informant does not make judgements concerning factors but records them all. Second, the informant is asked to record the details of verbal exchanges while they are taking place or as soon as they finish. This reduces the type of distortion that can occur in long term memory or when informants are asked about "ideal" cases. A number of informants said that they found the experience of completing language diaries stimulating because they became aware of the true nature of their language behaviour for the first time.

There are few observer problems of the type discussed by Labov (1970) since the observer is a genuine participant. The language diary also has the practical advantage of being cheap and comparatively simple to use. Students were able to complete language diaries successfully after only a few minutes of orientation to the task. The diary technique produced a considerable amount of usable information. The major restriction on its use elsewhere is the fairly high level of sophistication required of the informant, for example in understanding such concepts as "role".

An Accuracy Check

As a cross check on the accuracy of the reporting, three of the informants were asked both to complete the language diary, and also to record all their verbal exchanges on a portable cassette recorder (recorders and long playing cassette tapes were supplied). The language diaries were then checked against the recordings, in order to detect inaccuracies in the language diaries. These checked diaries were then compared to other language diaries to discover discrepancies and thus reveal informant bias. The results of this process were as follows. When the three diaries were compared to the tape recordings the codings were correct apart from one major discrepancy. This related to interactions with fellow university students of local Chinese backgrounds. Of 28 such interactions, 19 were recorded as taking place in Cantonese with some English admixture, 9 in pure Cantonese. When this was checked, English admixture was also found in 8 of these 9 interactions which supposedly took place in pure Cantonese. However, the amount of English was quite small in four of these, so in some cases a small quantity of English had been coded as a total absence (this variation in amount of English will be explored later). In situations where students were speaking to people they assumed to be Cantonese monolinguals, they spoke pure Cantonese without apparent difficulty.

RESEARCH ON LANGUAGE IN HONG KONG

Please tick appropriate boxes (√)

Name:

Subjects studied:

Secondary school(s) attended:

Languages spoken:

M ☐

Sex: F ☐

English ☐	Mandarin ☐
Cantonese ☐	Hakka ☐
Shanghainese ☐	Hoklo ☐
Chiu Chou ☐	Others (specify):

****

Notes for filling up the Language Diary

Please note down each time you speak, even if it is only to ask for a bus ticket. It is important that I know if you say " 兩 張 " or " 兩 張 " ticket".

Time

Please indicate the hour, and length of the conversation; e.g. 12.45 – 1.05 p.m. If you can't remember, just indicate roughly how long – e.g. 10 mins.

Situation

Give the place and circumstance, e.g. Canteen – lunch

Knowles Room 5–40 – seminar

Home – playing mah-jhong

Style

The way you were talking, e.g. friendly, angry criticism, amusing chat, serious discussion.

Subject

What you talked about, e.g. politics, your lectures, academic work, poverty, Mary's morals, drugs, etc.

Principal Speakers

Role – e.g. tutor, mother, stranger, fellow student, best friend, etc.

Education – please use the following codes:–

1 primary only

2E secondary English only

2C secondary Chinese only

3 tertiary (Polytechnic, University, etc.)

Sex – M or F

Age – approximately, e.g. 35–40

Background – Chinese = C, Western = W, Overseas Chinese = OC, Other.

Language

Please use the following codes:

1 Cantonese

2 Cantonese with English words

3 English

4 English with Cantonese words

Specify any other language, or mixture of languages, and give it a code number if you wish.

My grateful thanks for your help

Please return to John Gibbons.

18

Language Diary

| Time | Situation | | | | Principal Speakers | | | | | |
	Place	Circumstance	Style	Subject	Role	Education	Sex	Age	Background	Language (and comments)
5.00–5.15pm	Bus	way to City Hall	friendly	Eng. Drama & Misc. Chat	Fellow Student	3	M	20	C	1
5.15–5.30pm	Central District	way to City Hall	friendly	Eng. Dramatist: Osborne	Fellow Student	3	M	20	C	1
5.30–6.00pm	City Hall Library	borrowing books	friendly	books	Fellow Student	3	M	20	C	1
6.10–6.17pm	Ferry	on the way home	friendly	our friends	friend	2E	M	23–25	C	1
6.40–7.00pm	home	reading newspaper	amusing chat	news & TV prog.	aunt	–	F	63	C	Hakka
7.00–7.30pm	home	dinner	amusing chat	TV prog.; work; family chat	aunt, sisters nephews & nieces	– to 3	M & F	4– 63	C	Hakka (with aunt & sisters) 1 (with nephews & nieces)
8.30–8.37pm	home	helping nephew to do his homework	discussion	homework	nephew	2E	M	13	C	1
9.40pm	home	telling me to answer the phone	friendly	to answer the phone	aunt	–	F	63	C	Hakka

Language Diary (continued)

	Situation				Principal Speakers					
Time	Place	Circumstance	Style	Subject	Role	Education	Sex	Age	Background	Language (and comments)
9.40–9.45pm	home	answering the phone call	friend	an appointment to meet old friends	friend	2E	M	26	C	1
9.45–10.00pm	home	watching TV	friendly	TV prog. & family chat	aunt; sisters; brother-in-law; nephews & nieces	– to 3	M & F	13–63	C	1 & Hakka
11.50pm	home	reading	friendly	if I want something to eat before going to bed	aunt	–	F	63	C	Hakka
7.10–7.30am	bus	on the way to University	friendly	lectures	fellow student	3	M	20–22	C	2
7.30–7.40am	ferry	on the way to University	friendly	how to prepare for the May exam	fellow student	3	M	20–22	C	2
7.45–8.05am	bus	on the way to University	friendly	the Mencius	fellow student	3	M	20–22	C	2

Language Diary (continued)

| Time | Situation | | | | Principal Speakers | | | | | |
	Place	Circumstance	Style	Subject	Role	Education	Sex	Age	Background	Language (and comments)
8.20–8.27am	Main Bldg. 112	before lecture	friendly discussion	translation	fellow student	3	M & F	19–24	C	2
9.40–10.00am	Canteen	refreshments	"	translation & Eng. Novel of 1950's	"	3	M	19–21	C	2
10.05–10.15am	U. Bank	money-changing (coins)	friendly	money-changing	clerk	2	F	25	C	1
10.30–11.30am	U. Library	photocopying	friendly	the photocopying & photocopied materials	fellow students	3	M	19–21	C	1
1.10–1.30pm	Canteen	lunch	friendly	phonetics & misc. chat	fellow student	3	M	20	C	1
2.00–2.30pm	Old Halls	meeting of a group of fellow students	friendly discussion	translation & phonetics	fellow students	3	M & F	19–22	C	2

21

When these verified language diaries were compared with the remainder, there was no detectable difference in the nature of the entries. One of the verified diaries, however, had considerably more entries than most of the others, which may indicate some under-reporting.

The Sample

Characteristics

The sample numbered 27 informants, 14 female and 13 male. They were from the Faculties of Arts, Social Science and Science. Since the language diaries involved considerable (unpaid) effort on the part of students, these volunteers were obtained through personal contacts. It did not prove possible to obtain more volunteers, nor informants from other faculties. These informants contributed records of 431 verbal exchanges. The term "verbal exchange" is used to refer to an entry on a language diary, since many of these were too short to be called "conversations".

Speech Repertoire

All the students sampled have in their speech repertoire four codes. These are Cantonese, English and two types of mixture of Cantonese and English. One of the mixtures (referred to below as "MIX") is described in Chapter 3 as being partially koinéised; it is built on an essentially Cantonese base, with influences from English. The second mixture shows the reverse situation, where students speak English essentially, with some elements from Cantonese; this is referred to below as "English with Cantonese". The speech repertoire of all the students sampled therefore contains the following:

Cantonese   Mix   English-with-Cantonese   English

In addition comparatively small numbers of students speak other languages. These include Mandarin, Chinese Dialects other than Cantonese, and modern European languages other than English. There is also the occasional student who speaks another unusual language (e.g. Malay). Finally, it is possible to mix certain of these languages, especially for metalinguistic and teaching purposes in foreign language classes. So the potential other codes are:

Mandarin	Other Chinese Dialects	Other European Languages	Other Languages	Other Mixtures

In the sample that this research is investigating there were no cases of the use of pure European languages, no "other languages", and the only other Chinese dialect that occurred was Hakka. There would unquestionably have been other Chinese dialects such as Shanghainese and Hoklo if the sample had been larger. The numbers of exchanges in each language were as follows:

TABLE 2

Cantonese	... 171
Mix	... 191
English-with-Cantonese	... 11
English	... 42
Mandarin	... 5
Hakka	... 5
Other Mixtures	... 6

There is only one example of each of these "other mixtures" and they display no patterning, so they will be disregarded in the rest of the discussion.

Coding the Data

Owing to the large numbers of verbal exchanges, of factors, and in some cases, of variables within these factors, it proved necessary to use a computer to process the data. To make this possible, it was necessary to transform the data into numerical codes. (For details see Gibbons, 1983: Appendix 2.) A conservative policy was adopted, in which dubious cases were categorized as "missing values".

As an informal check on the coding procedure, 2 local Chinese and one Westerner were asked to code a section (19 verbal exchanges) of a language diary, using codes and coding sheets.[1] There was a total of 8 differences or uncertainties in coding compared to the master coding done by the researcher, i.e. less than 1%, and these were to do with topic (4), circumstance (2), and role (2).

Data Analysis (Non-Probabilistic)

Method

Once the data had been coded, they were processed by running large numbers of cross-tabulations, using the Statistical Package for the Social

Sciences, Mark V. Tables were printed out by the computer in which the possible code choices formed one axis, and a factor which might influence the choice of code formed the other axis. This was done repeatedly with the range of factors until one was found which explained a code choice (or nearly did so). When a factor explained nearly all cases, the unexplained cases were examined to see if they were identifiably exceptional. Once a code choice was explained, it could be eliminated from further consideration by the use of the *select if* command of the computer package, and the process repeated on the remaining data. This process required hand evaluation of hundreds of cross-tabulations: researchers who wish to process this type of data nowadays have available computer programmes which obviate this laborious sorting.

Model

The model used here is the widely used decision tree. For the advantages and problems of this type of model, see above.

Results

The findings produced by the cross-tabulations are displayed in summarized form in Figure 3, and discussed in the pages which follow.

Interlocutor's Background

As can be seen there were no occurrences of European languages and there were not sufficient examples of speech with Overseas Chinese for any significant pattern to emerge. A single contact with a non-local Asian was in English, which is predictable, since it is likely to be the only language that a Hong Kong Chinese would have in common with such a person. The fact that all encounters with Westerners took place in English (except one, which will be mentioned below) is by no means entirely predictable. Nearly all the Westerners in question are University staff, of whom a significant proportion speak Cantonese to a greater or lesser extent. The students must be aware of this in some cases. Nevertheless it seems that H.K.U. students nearly always speak to Westerners in English. The constraint in this case is presumably some type of social rule. The research confirms the impression of many Westerners with whom I have discussed the matter — that Chinese who know English are reluctant to speak Cantonese with Westerners, although Cantonese monolinguals are often delighted to speak Cantonese with foreigners. A similar situation is found in India, where

FIGURE 3   *Code choice tree*

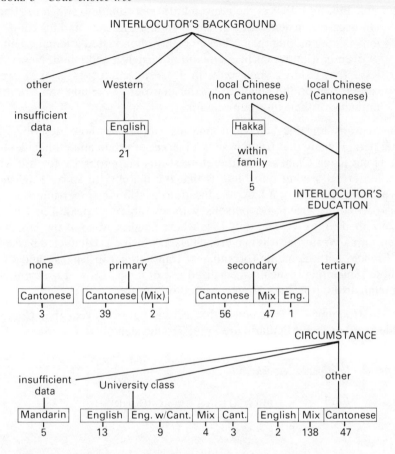

(The numbers on the tree are the actual number of verbal exchanges that took place in the language shown in the box above the number.)

Gumperz described the plight of American students of Hindi in the following terms: (Gumperz, 1966: 179):

"A typical difficulty, which is the subject of frequent complaints by returning students, concerns the lack of opportunity to use and practice the Hindi that had so laboriously been learned. Wherever the Westerner goes, in hotels, in shops, at parties, in public offices,

Indians address him in English. Their English may be barely intelligible but, nevertheless, he is given little opportunity to switch to Hindi. On occasion, when with a group of Indians, he may find his companions talking among themselves in highly abbreviated idiomatic Hindi, or even in what seems like a mixture of English and Hindi. Nevertheless, they address him only in English, almost as if they were capitalizing on the language barrier in order to exclude him from the intimacy of their in-group relations."

The reasons for this behaviour may be similar to those described by Gumperz, namely that Cantonese is a marker of group and ethnic identity for Hong Kong Chinese and therefore seems inappropriate for use with Westerners; a second possibility is that the inability to speak English is regarded as a mark of a lack of education, possibly membership of a low socio-economic group, so persons who are able to speak English are determined to do so. The only case where English was not the language used with a Westerner was in a French class, which was conducted basically in French, with elements (presumably translations) in English and Cantonese. Since this is such a specialized use of language, and is essentially metalinguistic, it has not been recorded on the tree.

In Chapter 1 it was noted that census figures reveal that Chinese dialects other than Mandarin are losing ground steadily to Cantonese. The

FIGURE 4   *Interlocutor's background*

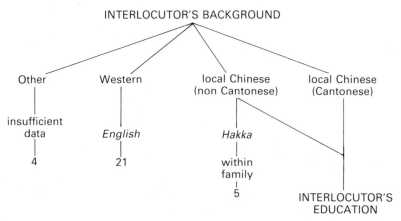

(The most decisive factor initially was the background ethnicity of the interlocutor.)

very low number of exchanges (5) in the "non-Cantonese speaking Chinese" category, despite the fact that there were 2 speakers of such dialects, provides supportive evidence. "Non-Cantonese" here means a local Chinese who speaks a dialect of Chinese other than Cantonese, although most speak Cantonese in addition. It happened that both non-Cantonese Chinese spoke Hakka. All the relevant encounters were with relatives in the students' own homes. One student records a single use of Hakka, at home, with her mother, to discuss "daily matters". Copies of the pages from the relevant language diary of the second student are given earlier in this chapter. It seems to be the case that the elderly aunt, and possibly the infant sister, are always addressed in Hakka, while the nephews and nieces are always addressed in Cantonese. With the other sisters it is not clear whether Cantonese is used in addition to Hakka. Nevertheless the entries on this diary seem to offer further evidence for language shift taking place among the non-Cantonese speaking Chinese of Hong Kong. The fact that the use of Hakka was limited to the family confirms the impression of the narrowing scope of use of dialects of Chinese other than Cantonese. Unfortunately there are insufficient data to give a list of factors which would consistently result in the choice of a non-Cantonese dialect when talking to a speaker of the same dialect, but it seems probable that the role and age of the interlocutor and the circumstance would be included in such a list. From the limited information available the language behaviour of the Hakka speakers with non-family seems indistinguishable from Cantonese native speakers.

Interlocutor's Education

When reference is made to "interlocutor's education" we are talking about the informant's perception of this factor.

It can be seen in Figure 5 that Cantonese speakers with no education are addressed only in Cantonese. The same holds true for those with only primary education, with only two exceptions where English was mixed in. These exceptions were (a) when a primary school student was being helped with English homework — essentially a metalinguistic use, and therefore to some extent standing outside the system; and (b) an "impure" situation, where both a University graduate, and a person with only primary education, were interlocutors, and it is not clear whether the informant used MIX with both people. Both exceptions are therefore questionable, and it seems fairly probable that there does exist some sort of general

FIGURE 5

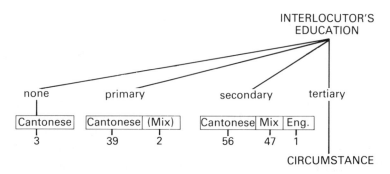

pattern, in which only Cantonese is used with persons who have primary education. This is by no means immediately predictable, since considerable emphasis is placed on English in Hong Kong's primary schools (see Tongue & Gibbons, 1982). It would be possible therefore for persons with primary education at least to mix in some English but this does not in fact happen. I have, however, heard persons with a low educational level mixing in the occasional word of English when speaking to someone of a similar level of education, but never when speaking to someone with a higher level of education (as the cross-tabulation reveals). One could speculate that this occasional word of English is "showing off" by displaying some knowledge of English, but the speaker would naturally avoid using English with someone who might reveal the limited nature of that knowledge.

The single use of English by a secondary educated local Chinese occurred when a student was singing Western "pop" songs with her brother. Western popular music is listened to by many young Hong Kong people, and some Cantonese language radio stations play large amounts (c.f. Chapter 1).

Although the choice tree groups together persons with secondary education, there is in fact a major difference in the codes used with persons who have had a Chinese medium secondary education, compared with those who have had an English medium secondary education. This can be shown by isolating the relevant variables in a cross-tabulation.

From Table 3 one can see that Hong Kong University students use a greater proportion of MIX to Cantonese with people who have received a secondary education in an (ostensibly) English medium school. The percentage of MIX used with such persons is approximately 63.5% as compared to 14.9% with people who have received a Chinese medium secondary education. This difference is not entirely surprising when one

TABLE 3 *Cross-Tabulation – Language used by interlocutor's secondary school type*

| | | Secondary school type | |
		Secondary Chinese	Secondary English
Language used	Cantonese	33	23
	Mix	7	40

takes into account the widespread use of MIX as a medium of instruction in ostensibly English medium schools (see Gibbons, 1982). Some use of MIX with people from Chinese medium secondary schools is not completely unexpected, since a reasonable English standard is required even in this type of school and, furthermore, some of the learning materials used in Chinese medium schools are in English (Gibbons, 1982: 124).

When the interlocutor has a tertiary education then *circumstance* becomes a decisive factor.

FIGURE 6

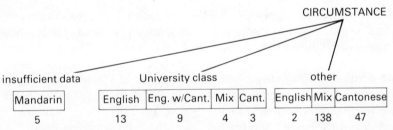

CIRCUMSTANCE

insufficient data	University class				other		
Mandarin	English	Eng. w/Cant.	Mix	Cant.	English	Mix	Cantonese
5	13	9	4	3	2	138	47

(*Note*: At this point in the tree interlocutors are limited to local Chinese with some tertiary education — mainly fellow students, see Figure 3.)

In practice, as shown in Figure 6, this factor served to distinguish university instruction from other situations. It was noted earlier that some problems arose in allocating codes in this factor "circumstance". This problem did not occur with the variable "University classes", since the information provided by the student in the place, time, circumstance and interlocutor columns placed the identity of the variable beyond doubt. This particular variable is important for two reasons:

(a) it is the only circumstance in which we find Cantonese inserted into a predominantly English discourse, and

(b) the majority of uses of English when speaking with fellow Chinese occurred in this circumstance.

Circumstance

The reason for this behaviour is that the University of Hong Kong is an English medium institution where the only officially permitted language of instruction is English with the exception of the study of other languages. In other words, English is used because there is an externally imposed rule that it must be used. The insertion into the predominantly English discourse of some elements of Cantonese by way of elucidation is not unexpected. One student provided examples of such insertions: they were abstract non-jargon terms such as "the politically aware" and "the survival of the fittest". Perhaps more surprising is the use of Cantonese and MIX in this circumstance. The figures are small and therefore not entirely trust-worthy; nevertheless, it appears that resistance to the use of English between Chinese people is sufficiently strong to quite frequently over-ride externally imposed rules favouring English.

The figures given under "other" circumstances are strong evidence of a social rule against members of this speech community using English when speaking to one another. The two uses of English are almost certainly rule violations, and will be discussed later.

This evidence coincides with the researcher's observations over eight years' working on this campus, i.e. students do not hold conversations in English with fellow Chinese unless compelled to do so. There are a number of insult terms which are used to describe Chinese who speak English to one another. These include "sā chàhn" "chàhn (hēi)" and "mouh sī" which mean a person is pretentious, "showing off" (an interesting reflection of the prestige attached to a knowledge of English), "faan wai" and "jok ngáuh" which mean "it turns my stomach", and strongest of all "suhng yéuhng" — literally "admires the West" (c.f. "nigger lover").

This social rule stigmatizes the use of English among Chinese who speak it reasonably well (or very well). It is at variance with social rules which operate in Singapore (see Crewe, 1977, in particular the article by Chia; and Platt, 1977), Kenya (Whiteley, 1974; Scotton, 1976), Uganda (Parkin, 1971), and India (Das Gupta, 1980). In these countries speakers who share an indigenous *lingua franca* nevertheless use the English component of their speech repertoire to express certain social meanings or to discuss certain topics. The interesting question here is why is this student speech community different? This question will be explored in Chapter 6.

The two exceptions to this rule both occurred in the privacy of the students' own homes. Although, on the basis of its rarity, the use of English among Chinese is abnormal, no motivation was apparent in one case. A student was watching television with her brother, and they discussed the plight of the heroine in English (it may be that they were watching English language television). In the other case a student was talking on the telephone to a friend. The interlocutor was an old friend from her élite westernized school. Although clearly an exception when contrasted with the 185 other interactions which avoided English, a possible interpretation will be given to this code choice in Chapter 7, after the social meaning of such behaviour has been examined.

Evaluating the Approach

A macro-sociolinguistic approach was used in this part of the investigation. It included most of the elements in Fishman's "Sociology of Language" model, in other words it asked "who speaks what language to whom, when and where?". It also included factors mentioned in Ervin-Tripp's (1964) model of the interaction of language topic and listener, and in Hymes' "ethnography of speaking" approach. What light is thrown on the macro-sociolinguistic approach by its use in practice?

Weak and Strong Claims for Macro-Sociolinguistic Models

In the sociolinguistic literature it is possible to find both "weak" and "strong" claims made for macro-sociolinguistic models. In the earlier "strong" models a range of factors *determined* the choice of a code, and speakers were "social automata" (Giles & Powesland, 1975). The later, more cautious "weak" claim was that these factors exert a strong influence upon rather than determine language behaviour (see for example Scotton & Ury, 1977; and Hymes, 1977).

This research supports the weaker model, in that there appear to be some cases where norms for code choice are deliberately violated by individuals for effect: a particularly striking example is the use of English by two girls from an élite school.

A second problem with the strong model is that it appears to presume that speakers will simply choose either one code or another in a given set of circumstances. In fact, speakers may not be entirely consistent in their behaviour, particularly when there are competing pressures for different codes. A case in point is the range of codes used in University classes: there is a general externally imposed University regulation that English will be used in classes: on the other hand there appears to be a social norm that stigmatizes the use of spoken English among Chinese. The consequence is a confused situation where English, Cantonese and both types of mixture are found.

The Importance of the Characteristics of the Participants

The macro-sociolinguistic approach to code choice includes the identity of the participants as a major factor. This is fully justified by the results, since ethnicity, family membership and education of the interlocutor comprise three of the four decisive factors in the choice tree.

Omission of the Language Competences of the Participants

Most macro-sociolinguistic field work shows an awareness of the relevance of the language competences, that is the level of ability of participants in a social encounter to speak languages (e.g. Trudgill & Tzavaras, 1977; McClure & Wentz, 1975: 421; and Jackson, 1974). However, many theoretical macro-sociolinguistic models of code choice omit this factor. It is not included in Ervin-Tripp's (1964) model, nor in Hymes' models — e.g. Hymes (1967) "Models of the Interaction of Language and social setting" and Hymes (1977), nor in Fishman's (1965) and (1971b) models, all of which look at variables involved in code choice. Yet it is obvious that the language competences of the participants can affect code choice: in this study university students do not speak to illiterates in English or mixed languages, because they will not understand them. Hymes (personal communication) writes that he considers it correct to consider the language competences of participants as a factor and that he would accommodate that factor in his category "what is done".

The factors included in the standard macro-sociolinguistic models generally exert their influence by the social consensus of the speech community — this is often referred to as "social norms". In contrast, the influence upon code choice of the language competences of participants derives from more pragmatic considerations of communicative efficacy: in basic terms, it is of limited use to attempt communication with a person in a language that he or she does not know. This type of pressure on code choice might be classified as "external" in comparison with the "internal" social norms.

Another type of "external" influence on code choice appeared in the behaviour of this speech community. This was a University regulation which imposed English as the language of University instruction. Such regulation of code choice by a higher authority is not uncommon. For example, it is particularly widespread in education systems, see Pascasio (1977) for the Philippines or the unfortunate history of the Gaelic languages in Britain and the "patois" in France. Another example is the phenomenon of the "official" governmental language, widely discussed in "language planning", for example Rubin & Jernudd (1972) and the tendentious Indian case (Das Gupta, 1980). A similar constraint on code choice is the "house rule" found in many major companies: some Swedish companies use English for internal communication, and Jardine, a major Hong Kong trading house, insists on the use of English for all written communications. All the examples constitute regulation of code choice by a higher authority, not always with the consent of the group on which the regulations are imposed.

As a consequence of the above, a complete model of code choice would include both "internal" or social influences, and "external" constraints, including *pragmatic* constraints such as the language competences of the participants and *imposed* constraints such as house rules.

The Absence of a Direct Link between Code Choice, and Time and Place

When the processing of the data began, a determined effort was made to investigate the relationship between code choice, and the setting in time and place, since, as we have seen, these form a major part of both sociology of language and ethnography of speaking models. Contrary to expectations, no such relationship was found. For example, one might have predicted the use of English in class *rooms* at class *hours*. On closer examination, however, it became apparent that the lecturers, if Chinese, would often chat to students in MIX during the times when actual instruction was not taking place, for example at the beginning and end of classes. English occurred only (but not always) when teaching began. In other words it was the social event "university instruction" which was associated with English, rather than physical or temporal factors.

There is no doubt that place and time can be successfully correlated with code choice, but it may be that this is a secondary effect of the social situation. Take, for example, the use of church Latin until comparatively recently. Presumably Roman Catholic churches and Sunday would correlate highly with the use of church Latin. The relationship is, however, an indirect one. The use of church Latin is directly related to religious services. These services often take place on Sunday in church, but there is no necessity for this as weekday masses and open air services illustrate. It is not the bricks and mortar, not the hour, but the human and social institutions, behaviour and beliefs that shape the language behaviour: these institutions, etc. can be associated with time and place on the one hand, and language on the other, but the association of language with time and place is essentially secondary and potentially misleading. Another well known example is Goffman's waiter, moving from kitchen to dining-room, and entirely changing his behaviour (Goffman, 1971: Ch. 3, especially 123–24). However, it is not the room that produces the difference, but the change in role, which in turn *is* influenced by the room. Presumably the waiter would not significantly modify his behaviour on moving from kitchen to dining room if the restaurant were closed and empty: it is the change of role, from one among equals to waiter, that shapes his behaviour.

On some occasions a place may appear to produce a code shift that is not related to social situation — for example, that awe that many people feel on first seeing the Grand Canyon may be reflected in their speech. However, in this case it seems probable that it is the psychological state "awe" (presumably experienced in other places) that is the direct influence on the code choice, so once again the relationship of place with code choice is secondary.

To summarize, in many cases it appears that time and place are associated with social situation and psychological state, and in turn, these are associated with code choice. Consequently, in such cases, the influences of time and place on code choice is secondary. In diagrammatic form:

TIME		SOCIAL SITUATION ·		CODE
	influence		influence	
PLACE	⟶	PSYCHOLOGICAL STATE	⟶	CHOICE

It would clearly be dangerously extreme to claim that setting never directly influences code choice. On the other hand, this factor may have been over-emphasized in macro-sociolinguistic sociology of language models, because insufficient recognition was given to the possible role of mediating social and psychological factors.

Summary

The findings of this part of the research lend support to a "weak" (rather than deterministic) macro-sociolinguistic model of code choice. Such a model would take particular note of the characteristics of participants, and "external" pressures such as regulations on code use, and the language competences of the participants. The setting in space and time would be carefully questioned and probably omitted as a factor of direct relevance. Instead, there would be an intervening level of social and psychological variables. A model of this type is discussed in Chapter 7.

Further Steps

There are two major areas that this initial study has left untouched. The first is the choice between MIX and Cantonese when conversing with a fellow Chinese with secondary education or above. It proved impossible to identify a single factor which explained this choice, and it was also the case that no combination of factors using this simple technique could be shown to be decisive. However, it was apparent that there were probabilistic relationships between various of the factors and the choice of MIX or Cantonese. For this reason a statistical study was undertaken (reported in the section which follows).

The second major question left unanswered was "why?". What is the motivation for the choice of certain codes in certain circumstances with certain types of interlocutor. In particular, why is spoken English so little used among Chinese, when it is a potential choice within their code repertoire. This will be explored in Chapter 6.

Statistically Re-analysing the Data

The code choices that remain unexplained on the decision tree are mostly between Cantonese and MIX. The cross-tabulation form of data processing afforded glimpses of combinations of factors which seemed to correlate with one code or the other, but there were no decisive variables, and this technique does not provide a way of evaluating the significance of correlations. To cope with this type of probabilistic data from the language diaries, a statistical model was applied. The purpose was to determine whether there were probabilistic relationships between any of the macro-sociolinguistic factors, and the individual's propensity to choose Cantonese or MIX. Collett developed and applied such a form of analysis, which is described in Appendix 3.[2]

Collett's approach takes account of an underlying problem in the processing of real language data. Since such data are not gathered in an experimental situation, it is not possible to rotate variables so as to eliminate the influence of one variable upon another. Consequently statistical models used to process the data (usually, as in this case, logistic models) do not provide findings whose probability can be measured. This applies to the model used here, and the one in Chapter 5.

The Data

The coded records derived from the language diaries (which had been previously used in the cross-tabulations) formed the basis for the statistical analysis. This analysis is concerned solely with cases where Cantonese and MIX are used with local Chinese with secondary education or above; therefore only such cases were included in the data for analysis. There were 295 such cases. Fifteen of these were deleted because of an excess of missing values, leaving a total data base of records of 280 verbal interactions. The number of cases is not particularly large, and the number of factors and the number of variables within each factor are considerable. To make statistical analysis viable, a number of the variables were regrouped to reduce their numbers. The factors and variables used in the analysis were the following:

Language Used The language used during the interaction. A choice of Cantonese (1) and MIX (2).

Reporter's School Type Schools were divided into four groups, running from most prestigious (1) to least prestigious (4). The groupings were obtained by administering an informal questionnaire to twenty university colleagues. One hypothesis is that MIX would be used more by students from more prestigious schools.

Reporter's Sex The sex of the student who completed the diary, male (1) or female (2). This factor might interact with the sex of the interlocutor.

Circumstance The type of activity that the participants are engaged in. They were grouped as follows: University class (1); leisure (2); private life (3); business (4); Chinese class (5); and student life (6).

Style The style of the conversation, from formal (1) to intimate (5).

Topic The topics were grouped as follows: University life (1); world view and affairs (2); non-family non-student leisure (3); everyday matters (4); family affairs (5).

Interlocutor's Sex The sex of the person to whom the reporter is speaking – male (1) or female (2).

Interlocutor's Age Divided into non-peer (1) – ages 1–11 and over 25; and peer (2) – 12–24.

Place The place where the interaction took place. Home (1); elsewhere public (2); elsewhere private (3); and university (4).

The emphasis placed on public versus private here results from a general impression given by the language diaries, that social rules appear to exert less pressure in private.

Results

First the nine factors were fitted to deviances. The value of the deviance near its degree of freedom indicates a good "fit", i.e. it is likely that the factors included in the model can explain some of the variation (see Appendix 3). In this particular case it means that the lower the deviance is, the more probable it is that the factor influences the choice between MIX and Cantonese.

From Table 4 it is clear that the Interlocutor's Age and the Topic are the most important single variables since their deviances are nearest their degree of freedom. Place may also be important.

TABLE 4

Factor Fitted	Deviance	Degrees of Freedom
Mean	362.57	279
Reporter's School	358.54	276
Reporter's Sex	361.58	278
Circumstance	358.37	274
Style	360.63	275
Topic	316.96	274
Interlocutor's Sex	359.16	277
Interlocutor's Age	326.63	278
Place	341.14	276

The second step was to try a large number of combinations of variables. Here one is attempting to fit a model of combinations of factors, to find the best explanation for the variation in choice between MIX and Cantonese. The most important findings are given in Table 5. The table in turn is followed by comments on the various combinations.

The final model, as seen in Table 5, gives a deviance almost equal to its degree of freedom, so is a good fit to the data. This means that, using this data, the choice between Cantonese and MIX is probably influenced by a combination of three main factors; the style of the conversation, the age of interlocutors, and the topic of the conversation. There is also an interaction effect between the topic and the style of the talk.

Having discovered which combination of variables best explains the variation, we next need to ask the direction in which these influences

TABLE 5

Model	Deviance	Degrees of Freedom	Comment
Interlocutor's Age + Topic	293.60	273	
Interlocutor's Age + Topic + Place	290.24	270	1
Interlocutor's Age + Place	312.59	275	2
Interlocutor's Age + Topic + Reporter's Sex	290.64	272	3
Interlocutor's Age + Topic + Rep. Sex + Int. Sex	290.38	270	3
Interlocutor's Age + Topic + Rep. Sex × Int. Sex	287.34	268	3
Topic + Style + Interlocutor's Age	290.06	269	4
Topic + Style + Interlocutor's Age + Style × Topic	263.64	258	5

Comments
1. Place need not be included in the model, as it produces no improvement when placed alongside the Interlocutor's Age and the Topic.
2. The Topic is important along with the Interlocutor's Age – its omission produces a much less good fit.
3. The Reporter's Sex, the Interlocutor's Sex and their interaction are not relevant.
4. These figures provide little evidence that Style is needed in addition to the Topic and the Interlocutor's Age, however –
5. the interaction of Topic and Style is important in handling some of the remaining variation, so both main effects need to be in the model.

operate. Are speakers more likely to use MIX or Cantonese with peers? to discuss family affairs? Looking at the variables in turn, we can see the direction in which they influence the code choice. Table 6 provides estimated values of the effects of the various levels of style. The higher the positive number, the more likely it is that the speakers will use MIX.

TABLE 6   *Effects of different levels of style*

Variable	Estimated Value
population mean	−0.405
Style 1 (most formal)	0.000
Style 2	0.514
Style 3	0.379
Style 4	0.964
Style 5 (least formal)	6.996

Since the estimated effects increase from zero to 6.996 in order (apart from variables 2, 3), the probability of use of MIX increases as the conversation becomes less formal.

Turning to the influence of Topic upon code choice, the larger the negative number, the more likely it is that speakers will use Cantonese. However, since there were problems in the coding of Topic, the figures are not entirely reliable (see Table 7).

TABLE 7   *Effects of different topics*

Variable	Estimated Value
Topic 1 (University life)	0.000
Topic 2 (world view)	−1.984
Topic 3 (leisure activities)	−17.793
Topic 4 (every day matters)	−2.167
Topic 5 (family affairs)	−1.046
(Topic 6 (missing values)	−7.404)

The main conclusion that can be drawn from this table is that University life is more likely to be discussed in MIX, while non-University leisure activity is more likely to be discussed in Cantonese.

Turning to the remaining major factor, the Interlocutor's Age, this result is displayed in Table 8.

TABLE 8   *Effects of age*

Variable	Estimated Value
1 (non-peer)	0.000
2 (peer)	1.636

It can be seen from this that MIX is more likely to be spoken with peers than with non-peers.

In summary therefore, we can say that the likelihood of MIX being used rather than Cantonese increases in the following conditions:

1. the interlocutor is close in age to the student – i.e. is of the peer age group.
2. the style of the interaction is informal.
3. the topic is University life.

Factors which do *not* appear to influence this code choice are the sex of speakers, the prestige of the interlocutor's schooling, the circumstance, or the place.

Evaluation of a Statistical Approach

Macro-sociolinguistic theory has tended to assume that a single code choice results from a given set of factors such as topic, participants, and social event (see the introduction to this chapter). As we have already noted there are practical grounds for questioning this. In fact many macro-sociolinguistic surveys have used probabilistic techniques in the analysis of code choice — see for example Fishman *et al.* (1971) and Scotton (1976). While probabilistic approaches are integral to micro-sociolinguistics, particularly of the Labov type, they have yet to find a place in core macro-sociolinguistic theory. Yet, as our data have shown, it is rare to find total conformity in code choice — variation exists. While this research has revealed external constraints on code choice, and distinct social rules governing the use of English with Chinese and Westerners, other code choices are not clear cut. This implies that a more complete model might include both simple choices governed by external constraints or social rules, and variation in circumstances where the acceptability of code choices is high, low or indeterminate. These varying degrees of acceptability may best be described in terms of pressure from various factors to choose or not to choose certain codes. (If sampling is adequate) it may be possible to relate a degree of pressure or influence to each individual factor (such as participants, topic, etc.) and to arrive at a model in which one can predict code choice in probabilistic terms according to the prevalent factors. The lack of an absolute decision about code might be seen as a result of competing pressures from different factors. The probabilistic model used in this chapter demonstrates the potential usefulness of such a system to describe code choice. So probability, not just simple decision, can form part of future macro-sociolinguistic models of code choice.

The Next Steps

This statistical study has revealed the role of age, style and topic in the choice between Cantonese and MIX. We noted, however, that two elements still require clarification. First, the coding of "topic" was not always satisfactory, so some kind of follow-up procedures are needed.

Secondly, there were indications that subjects were not entirely accurate in their assignation of their speech to the categories of Cantonese and MIX: this problem is not helped toward a solution by the lack of information in the survey concerning the mixing process. Both problems derive from the necessarily imprecise nature of a broad initial survey. The purpose of such surveys is normally to gain a general rather than a detailed picture (see the introduction to this chapter). Such macro-surveys raise questions and indicate areas that can form the focus of more precise study, in which "micro" techniques are required. One question, concerning the motivation for code choice, has already appeared. Another area which seems to require more detailed study is the nature of MIX, and the (possibly consequent) confused boundary between MIX and Cantonese. Once the nature of MIX has been explored (Chapter 3) code choice within this area can be studied in a more sensitive fashion.

Notes to Chapter 2

1. I should like to thank Paula Fleming. Wong Hok Chun and Yip Koon Hung for this service.
2. I should like to express my gratitude to Dr Collett of the Centre for Applied Statistics, University of Reading, without whose help this part of the research would have been impossible.

3 A Description of Salient Linguistic Characteristics of "MIX"

Introduction

This chapter is an attempt to *characterize* MIX for two purposes. The first purpose relates principally to the discussion in Chapter 2, and is an attempt to discover to what extent MIX can be treated as an alternative code choice rather than simply as rapid Cantonese–English code-switching. To this end at various linguistic levels there are descriptions of autonomous features of MIX. The second purpose is to make possible an analysis of the variation in the composition of MIX as this relates to such sociolinguistic variables as the sex and schooling of the subject (see Chapter 4). Neither purpose demands exhaustive linguistic analysis of MIX (a book in itself), but rather a linguistic description of distinctive characteristics (for purpose 1) and of the composition of MIX (for purpose 2). The description which follows attempts to serve these purposes by briefly examining MIX at a number of levels, including segmental and suprasegmental phonology, syntax and lexis. It is based on substantial recordings of conversations among students, which are described in the following section.

The Data Base

The data base for chapters 3–5 consists of tape recordings of authentic student conversations. As part of their course work, students were asked to tape record a segment of natural conversation with fellow students. The recordings varied in length from three minutes to more than one hour. The student who made the recording was also required to transcribe the first ten minutes of it. This avoided problems related to the transcription of authentic conversation by persons not present during the conversation. The students were provided with small unobtrusive battery-powered Sony

42

cassette recorders with built-in microphones, and cassettes. The quality of the recording was in most cases quite good, but not adequate for Labovian studies of fine phonetic variation. There were 29 recordings in all. They involved 85 participants, 41 male, 43 female, and one not known. The student informants were also requested to supply the following information on themselves and other participants: (1) last secondary school attended (2) Faculty (3) subjects studied at University. This information was provided for most speakers, although occasionally the informant was uncertain of the details of a participant (for example someone who joined a conversation in the student canteen), and failed to ask him or her for details. The conversations took place in various parts of the campus, predominantly in the student canteen and in halls of residence. Student informants say that the conversations sound natural, apart from some natural inhibition in the first few utterances on some tapes. The composition of the sample by Faculty is as follows: Arts – 70; Social Science – 9; Medicine – 4; Law – 2. The findings can therefore be seen to relate more definitely to Arts students, although the size of the Social Science representation, and the fact that the Faculties of Arts and Social Science share many students may make the findings relevant to Social Science students also. It would be impractical to include the entire data base here. A transcription of a representative recording is available in Appendix I. Where possible an example will be given from this recording, and such examples are asterisked. The reader is urged to look at this transcription to gain a "feel" for MIX before reading on.

This description will be undertaken at a number of levels, including pronunciation, grammar and word meaning. Within each level we shall see elements that form part of the systems of the two contributing languages (English and Cantonese), and elements that do not form part of either language and can therefore be viewed as distinct.

In the sample of MIX which was used for this study Cantonese is dominant at all linguistic levels; in the terminology of Poplack (1980) and Huerta (1978) Cantonese is the "base language". Evidence the fact that in the syllable counts described in Chapter 5, the mean proportion of Cantonese is around 85–90% of the syllables. The Cantonese element in MIX appears to have undergone little modification — its pronunciation, grammar and vocabulary appear virtually identical to monolingual Cantonese speech. It is the English contribution to MIX which has been modified and adapted in a number of interesting ways, and which will form the focus of the description, along with the autonomous elements mentioned in the preceding paragraph.

These English items should be distinguished from the quite numerous English borrowings found in the speech of Hong Kong Cantonese monolinguals which have been entirely assimilated to Cantonese norms. The English elements referred to in this chapter are used almost exclusively by English — Cantonese bilinguals, and few have a written Chinese form.

Throughout this chapter there is a distinction made between well integrated and less integrated items. The categories are not truly discrete, but their usefulness for descriptive purposes will hopefully emerge from the description.

Modification of English Segmentals

The modification in MIX of English vowels, and of final and initial consonants and consonant clusters will be discussed in turn. Modifications to these segments are categorized into "substitution", "deletion", "addition" and "systematic retention". The categories are defined below.

Substitution – When a speaker is using a second language, there is a well attested tendency to assimilate the segmentals of that language towards equivalents in his native language (see Weinreich, 1974). They need not be the nearest in acoustic terms, but rather ones that occupy a similar contrastive position in the sound system of the speaker's native language. This process can be complete, when one can say that "substitution" has taken place, or it can be a partial movement, in which case there may be "continua" in pronunciation between the two languages. Such continua in pronunciation range from near native English to totally Cantonese. These are, however, difficult to document in single cases, since there is often a possible explanation for modifications in the phonetic environment, and as was noted previously the quality of the recording rarely permits fine phonetic analysis.

Deletion – One or more English segmentals are lost.

Addition – A segmental is added.

In addition there were some English forms which do not occur in Cantonese that were nonetheless consistently not modified. This type of patterning is referred to as *Systematic Retention*.

A Note on Cantonese Phonology[1]

Cantonese is normally taken to consist of morphemes with the underlying structure CVC. The initial C (consonant or consonant cluster) may consist of one of the following:

/ p p' t t' k k' ts ts' f h s l m n ŋ w k'w kw /

(the apostrophe represents aspiration).
The final –VC is a limited set consisting only of the following combinations
(after Cheung, 1972: 3).

	V + Ø	V + semivowel		V + nasal			V + stop	
ɑ	ɑ	ɑj	ɑw	ɑm	ɑn	ɑŋ	ɑp	ɑt	ɑk
a	*	aj	aw	am	an	aŋ	ap	at	ak
ɛ	ɛ	ɛj	*	*	*	ɛŋ	*	*	ɛk
œ	œ	œɥ	*	*	œn	œŋ	*	œt	œk
ɔ	ɔ	ɔj	ɔw	*	ɔn	ɔŋ	*	ɔt	ɔk
i	i	*	iw	im	in	iŋ	ip	it	ik
u	u	uj	*	*	un	uŋ	*	ut	uk
y	y	*	*	*	yn	*	*	yt	*

(Asterisks mark gaps in the system)

In Cheung's treatment possible final −C includes zero, /ɥ/and /j/realized as
[i], and /w/ realized as [u]. For a more complete description see Cheung
(1972: chapter 1) and Hashimoto (1972). For a description of English
phonology see Gimson (1970).

Vowels

Chan (1968) gives an exhaustive treatment of the differences between
the English and Cantonese vowel systems.

Substitution

This phenomenon is very common, but it is best and most unequivo-
cally illustrated by cases in which an English phonemic contrast is lost in
the MIX pronunciation. In the examples below one can clearly observe the
loss of the English /i/ − /i:/ contrast, because both are replaced by the
(slightly different) Cantonese /i/. (Examples are presented in three columns. To the left is the MIX pronunciation, in the middle the standard
British English "RP" pronunciation, following Jones, 1967, and to the
right the normal orthography. Asterisked examples are drawn from the
transcription in Appendix 1.)

[lit'ʊ]*   /litl/   "little"
[rits'it¹]   /ri'tri:t/   "retreat"
[ritsanœ^w]   /'ri:dʒənel/   "regional"
[t'w^εent'i p'ip'œu]*   /'twenti'pi:pl/   "twenty people"

The main change is in the pronunciation of English /i/ since it is considerably more distant from Cantonese /i/ in articulatory position.

A second case of substitution which can be clearly observed because it
leads to the loss of a contrast, can be seen in these examples:

[k'εm]   /kem/, /kæmp/   "chem" and "camp" *
[εk¹sεm]   /ig'zæm/, /ig'zempt/   "exam" and "exempt"
[k'ɔn sεp¹]   /'kɔnsept/   "concept"
[`k'ε,ri:]   /'kæri/   "carry"

It is evident, especially in the cases of [εk¹sεm] and [k'εm] — that the
English phonemes /e/ and /æ/ have been replaced by Cantonese /ε/ which
falls between them. The full loss of this contrast is most commonly found in
well integrated words; in less integrated words (see the next section) there
is a tendency towards "continua".

Addition

Examples:²

(fn.) [‾a:t¹′si]   /a:ts/   "arts"
      [‾ou –hɔ si]*   /'əuld 'hɔ:lz/   "Old Halls"
      [‾nou ˌsi]   /nəulz/   "Knowles"
      [‾tsɔk¹′ka:]   /dʒɔg/ abbreviation "geog." for /dʒɔgrəfi/ "geography"
      [ˌa:–fεi]*   /ə'fil/ abbreviation "affil." for /ə'filieitid/ "affiliated"

In the first three examples one can observe that students are using the well
documented Cantonese and pidgin English modification of English final /s/.
Since the latter is not a possible final consonant in Cantonese, this is one
strategy for adapting it to Cantonese norms. This is by no means a regular
phenomenon, the alternative forms [a:s] [ou hɔ]* and [nous] also occur in
the data. The other two examples of addition are less easily amenable to
explanation. [‾tsɔk¹ka:] has an additional [a:] and [–fεi] an additional [ε].
It is possible in the case of [‾tsɔk¹ka:] that the final voicing of (e) /dʒɔg/
has been realized as a vowel. In the case of [ˌa:-fεi] the provenance of the

additional [ɛ] is problematic, since it is not found in the English source; final /-l/ does not occur in Cantonese, and furthermore the syllables /fi/, /fim/, /fin/ and /fiŋ/ are absent, so this addition of /ɛ/ may be a modification to an existing Cantonese form. One should perhaps also mention the fact that words which in Mandarin have the pronunciation "consonant + /i/" may have the pronunciation "consonant + /ei/" in Cantonese, so [ˌa:–fɛi] may represent a generalization of this correspondence. The word [ˌa:–fɛi] is found on a number of different recordings, and appears to be common.

Deletion

[ts'ɛ]   /tʃɛə/   "chair"
[tsɔn]   /dʒɔin/   "join" (compare [tsɔn]*   /dʒɔn/ "John")

Vowels are lost comparatively rarely. In the examples given here /ɛə/ does not exist in Cantonese, and neither does the combination consonant – diphthong – consonant.

Systematic Retention

Here we are discussing cases where English systems are not transmuted into Cantonese equivalents, but are instead consistently retained intact.

[fɔm]   /fɔ:m/   "form"
[˗kɔm ⁻p'juˏ t'a:]   /kəm'pju:tə/   "computer"
[k'ɛm]*   /kæmp/   "camp"
[˗fi⁻lɔ]*   /fi'lɔ/   "philo" abbreviation for /fi'lɔsəfi/
                                        "philosophy"

In the examples to the left the combinations |ɔm| and |ɛm] are retained, although these are not found in Cantonese. The pressure on such combinations to modify towards Cantonese is induced by the fact that in secondary school "form" is pronounced [fɔŋ]. [˗fi⁻lɔ| is an extremely common MIX term with many occurrences on tape: there are no cases of a change to [˗fɛi ⁻lɔ], despite the case of [ˌa: –fɛi] discussed above. These cases might be regarded as essentially phonotactic. No examples of the systematic retention of English vowels other than this type were found.

Let us now see how these four processes are manifested in MIX consonants.

Single Initial Consonants

Substitution

When listening to recordings of student speech one perceives fairly soon that sets of English initial voiced consonants are replaced by similar sets of Cantonese unaspirated consonants; so in well assimilated words initial /b d g dʒ/ are consistently replaced by Cantonese unaspirated /p t k ts/ respectively. It is, however, difficult to find unassailable single examples since we may be talking of differences in micro-seconds of the onset of voicing. The following are among the least questionable:

[ˌɛnˊtsin]	/ˈendʒin/	"engine"
[ˌhai ⁻tˈɛiˌpou]	/ˈhai ˈteibl/	"high table"
[⁻tap¹ ˌpou]	/ˈdʌbl/	"double"

In each of these cases there is an English voiced consonant which falls between two other voiced elements. In English there is little or no diminution in voicing. However, in the form in which the corresponding consonants appear in the examples on the left, they are syllable initial, and there is a perceptible hiatus in voicing during the articulation of the consonant and before the onset of voicing for the following vowel.

Another area of interest is English /s/ and /ʃ/. Variants of the Cantonese /s/ lie between the two, being produced in many cases with only slight grooving and more palatalization than English /s/, but not taking on the full characteristics of /ʃ/. Variants of Cantonese /s/ come close to both English /s/ and /ʃ/. There is no opposition of the /ʃ/ – /s/ type in Cantonese. Examples

[faŋ sœn]	/ˈfʌŋkʃən/	"function"
[ma:sin]	/məˈʃiːn/	"machine"
[søt¹]	/səːt/	"cert." (certificate)
[ˋsouˌsi]	/ˈsəusi/	"soci." (sociology)

Single Final Consonants

There are very great differences in the range of acceptable final consonants between English and Cantonese. A major example is the lack of final non-nasal voiced consonants in Cantonese. One could therefore predict substantial reduction in English final consonants.

Substitution

[klap¹]	/klʌb/	"club"
[sap¹ tsik¹]	/'sʌbdʒikt/	"subject"
[ɛp¹ sœt¹ ti t'i]*	/əb'sə:diti/	"absurdity"
[mu:t¹]	/mu:d/	"mood"

In these cases there are three examples of final (e) /–b/, realized as [⁻p¹] and two of final (e)/–d/, realized as [–t¹]. Although some of these cases are possibly conditioned variants, the /b/ in "subject" falls between voiced segments, and would consequently be voiced in native English speech. There are few unequivocal cases of voiced final consonants on tape.

[ˌri – sœf]	/ri'zə:v/	"reserve"
[_a:̀ ts'if]	/ə'tʃi:v/	"achieve"
[ɛk¹ t'i v̂itis]	/æk'tivitiz/	"activities"

In these examples one can see that the devoicing also occurs in the English final fricative consonants /v/ and /z/. These are not strongly articulated (i.e. they are "lenis"), so they might be transcribed [v̥] and [z̥].

From this evidence there would appear to be a general tendency for final non-nasal single voiced consonants to be replaced by voiceless equivalents.

Addition

[_ɛp¹ˌplai]	/ə'plai/	"apply"
[⁻pɔp¹ ˌp'ju ˌla:]	/'pɔpjulə/	"popular"
[ˌlɛt¹ˋt'a]	/'letə/	"letter"
[⁻k'ap¹ˋfa:]	/'kʌvə/	"cover"

In the above examples one can observe a process akin to gemination, in which a final consonant is added to the end of each of the initial consonants.

Deletion

[ˌhɔ]	/hɔ:l/	"hall"
[rɔu]*	/rəul/	"roll"
[kɔ:]*	/kɔ:l/	"call"
[fimɛiu]*	/fi: meil/	"female"

In these examples one can see that /əu/ has become [ɔu] as in previous examples, and that the final (e) /–1/ has been lost. There is no final /1/ in Cantonese, and in fast colloquial English native speech there is a tendency for /1/ to be vocalized in this environment. The word [ˌhɔ] occurred many times, and was consistently pronounced in this way. There are other unpatterned deletions such as:

[−pai ⁻la]	/bai' lʌk/	"by luck"
['krɛi]	/greid/	"grade"
[t'ɛ]	/teik/	"take" (found only once: [t'ɛik¹] found 16 times)

Systematic Retention

Retention of impermissible final vowel plus /m/ combinations has already been mentioned. One might add the case of [k'ɛm] "chemistry" – in which the final [ɛm] is consistently carried over from English, although this combination is not found in Cantonese.

Other examples are:

[laif]	/laif/	"life"
[ˌri-sœf]	/ri'zə:v/	"reserve"

Here we have, in the case of [laif], the retention of final (e) /–f/. In the second case we have both substitution and systemtic retention, since final /f/ is not found in Cantonese (see "substitution" above). There are no cases in which final /f/ is lost, and MIX rarely follows the normal Cantonese borrowing/pidgin English pattern of adding a /u/ sound to final (e) /–f/.

Initial Consonant Clusters

Cantonese has only the consonant clusters "consonant plus /j/" and "consonant plus /w/", and these are found solely in initial position. Some phonologists prefer to treat /w/ and /j/ as vowels and would say that there are no consonant clusters in Cantonese. The forms /ts/ and /ts'/ are normally treated as single segments, the second symbol representing the manner of release of the stop in a similar fashion to English /tʃ/. The following examples illustrate the situation with regard to the adaptation of (e) stop + /r,1/. We have examples where /r/, /1/ are retained, where they are lost, and in the case of "matric" a continuum from retention to replacement plus deletion. This represents fairly adequately the situation with regard to this type of cluster: namely a situation of unstable flux.

[p'ɛi]*	/plei/	"play"
[k'lous]*	/kləuz/	"close"
[əp'ɔk˧ si mœt˧ li]*	/ə'prɔksimətli/	"approximately"
[t'ruan]*	/'tru:ənt/	"truant"
[_mɛt˧⁻t'rik˧]		
[_mɛt˧⁻t'ˢʳik˧]	/mə'trik/	"matric."
[_mɛt˧⁻ts'ik˧]		

Systematic Retention

It can be seen in the following examples that syllable initial English /st/ is not simplified:

[k'ri stɔ:s]	/'kristəlz/	"crystals"
[stɛt˧]	/stæts/	"stats."
[steiʃœn]	/'steiʃən/	"station"
[hɔ stɔuʷ]*	/'hɔstəl/	"hostel"

Many other cases were found on tape; sufficient to say that this is regular behaviour. It contrasts with monolingual Cantonese borrowings and pidgin English, both of which introduce an /i/ between the two consonants, thus reducing the cluster, e.g.

/sitɔ/   "store"   /sitik/   "stick"

When questioned, student informants stated that a fellow student who employed such a strategy, and used a form such as *[si tɛt˧] for "stats." would be either misunderstood, or laughed at. This would appear to be a clear case of a distinct MIX norm. Note also these examples:

[spɔt˧]*	/spɔ:t/	"sport"
[sku]*	/sku:l/	"school"

Although there are insufficient data to generalize, the same may also apply to initial /sp/ and /sk/.

Final Consonant Clusters

There are no final consonant clusters in Cantonese, which results in pressure to reduce these clusters in various ways.

Deletion of one element

As in initial consonant clusters there is a tendency for one segmental to be lost. Examples are:

(e) /–st/ becomes [–s]
[fas]   /fɜ:st/   "first"
[a: kɛins]   /ə'genst/   "against"

(e) /–ks/ becomes [–s]
[sis]   /siks/   "six"
[ɛst'rim]   /ik'stri:m/   "extreme"

(e) /–ŋk/ becomes [–ŋ]
[⁻faŋ´søn]   /'fʌŋkʃn/   "function"

(e) /–nd/ becomes [–n]
[sɛ k'œn]   /'sekənd/   "second"
[ɛn]*   /ænd/   "and"

(e) /–nt/ becoms [–n]
[tok ju man]   /'dɔkjumənt/   "document"
[ɒɒin]*   /ɒɒint/   "ɛɔint"

This illustrates the elision of one consonant in the pair, but does not explain the source of the reduced forms. In other words we do not know why one member of the cluster rather than another is deleted consistently in the above cases and in many other parallel examples in the data. The work of Brown (1977: chapter 4) may give some help in solving this question. She discusses the manner in which in native English speech some segmentals are normally realized only in citation forms or very slow clear speech, but are reduced in a rule governed way in "fast informal" speech. She writes (pp. 60–61):

> "Another very common process in informal speech is elision — the 'missing' out of a consonant or vowel, or both, that would be present in the slow colloquial pronunciation of a word in isolation. As with assimilation the most common place to find consonant elision is at the end of a syllable. The most common consonants to find involved in elision are /t/ and /d/."

Brown mentions in particular the loss of /t/ in the environment {s–#C}, and she gives as examples ['fɜs 'θri:] "first three", and ['las 'jiə] "last year". Compare these losses of /t/ from the tape recordings of student speech (the first is particularly close to Brown's two examples):

[fas jia]	"firs*t* year"
[a keins] / k'œy /. . .	"agains*t* him"

One difference between student speech and the native English system described by Brown is that these pronunciations are consistently used regardless of the nature (or lack) of the following sound, so the environment in which /t/ can be omitted is {s–#}. So the term [a kɛins] is pronounced in this fashion by the community in all phonetic environments.

Brown describes the consistent omission of /d/ in the environment {n – #}, for example ['fɔ ' θauzən wə] "four thousand were" [a:lən 'trʌblz]" (Northern) Ireland troubles". Similarly on the tape recordings of student speech cases such as [sɛk'øn] "secon*d*" and [ɛn] "an*d*" were found. Unlike native speech (as described by Brown) this rule includes /t/ in this environment, e.g. [ɛlou k'wan] "eloquen*t*", [tɔkjuman] "documen*t*", [a sai man] "assignmen*t*". In English native speech these final /t/'s are often reduced to [ʔ], so a second interpretation is that a reduction is taken a stage further to become an omission.

In Brown's data /k/ is lost in native speech only in the environments {s–#} and {–s#}, and only in a limited number of words. A generalization of this rule to other words may explain student pronunciations such [ap'a sis] "upper si*x*" and [ɛst'rim] "e*x*treme".

Simplification of final consonant clusters is also well documented in American English (e.g. Luelsdorf, 1975: 52–58), with variation related to socio-demographic factors such as sex, age, class and ethnicity, as well as style (Wolfram, 1969: 57–82). In the examples given above there is consistent loss of the element(s) of the consonant cluster which Brown documents as being lost in fast native pronunciation, and no loss of the element(s) which would not be so reduced or lost. It seems possible therefore that the student community is simplifying some consonant clusters by the use and extension of native speaker rules. An alternative explanation is that this communality in the process of reduction in MIX and in two native varieties of English derives from a common pressure towards economy of effort in articulation.

Division

In MIX, English words are regularly segmented in clear conformity
with the phonotactics of the Cantonese morpheme, e.g.

[ɛk¹ sœ sais]	/ˈeksəsaiz/	"exercise"
[mɛk¹ si ma:]	/ˈmæksimə/	"maxima"
[pɛŋ kiŋ]	/ˈbæŋkiŋ/	"banking"
[pʼous tʼa:]	/ˈpəustə/	"poster"

The cumulative phonetic detail would appear to indicate juncture (with
varying degrees of clarity), suggesting that the English consonant clusters
are reduced by splitting them between syllables; the first member of the
cluster ends one syllable and the second begins the next. A related
phenomenon may be found in this example

[ta:ns̲]/a/   "dance" (plus particle)

Here the second segment of the consonant cluster is linked to the following
utterance particle.

Reduction by vowel addition

This can be observed in these examples.

[a:t¹ si]	/a:ts/	"arts"
[mɛt¹ si]	/mæθs/	"maths."

The addition of [i] follows the pattern of monolingual Cantonese borrowing. The addition effectively reduces the final consonant cluster.

Discussion

When elements from one language are embedded in another, one
would expect these elements to be influenced by the surrounding language.
If the surrounding language is also the native language, while these
elements are from a second language, experience might lead us to expect
even greater modifications. This phenomenon is attested in a number of
speech communities: for example Gumperz & Hernández–Chavez (1971:
319) remark:

"9.M: Pero como, you know ... la Estela ... The English form here
seems a regular part of the Spanish text, and this is signalled

phonetically by the fact that the pronunciation of the vowel *o* is relatively undiphthongised and thus differs from other instances of *o* in English passages. Similarly words like *ice cream* have Spanish-like pronunciations when they occur within Spanish texts, and English-like pronunciations in the English text."

We might therefore predict a very high level of movement towards the Cantonese phonological system in English elements used in a predominantly Cantonese environment. In many cases, this is indeed what occurs: we have observed the processes of substitution, addition and deletion working towards this end.

Nevertheless, the process is by means complete and consistent — there are many intermediate forms, and continua. Such phenomena have also been described in pidgin and creole studies, see for example Bickerton's (1975) "post creole continuum", and Hall (1966:31) discussing Neo-Melanesian pidgin.

At the end of the continuum that is nearest to Cantonese, we do not find the pure Cantonese system. Instead there is a compound system composed of the Cantonese phonological system plus a limited set of elements from English (discussed under "systematic retention" in the preceding section). This system, neither English nor Cantonese but an amalgam, is of some theoretical interest, and ramifications are discussed in the conclusion to this chapter.

Stress

There are two principal routes through which English lexis has traditionally been borrowed into Cantonese — writing and speech. When it is found necessary to produce a *written* Chinese version of foreign words, (often proper nouns), non-segmental features of the foreign word such as stress are largely ignored. For example, many Chinese street names in Hong Kong are clumsy (sometimes tortured) transliterations of English names, in which the consonants in a cluster are often each assigned a character (one syllable in speech). For example, the spoken Cantonese rendering of the Chinese name for "Belcher" (Street) is ˥pɛi˩lou ˉtsa:/.

When borrowings have come essentially through speech, however, a different form of phonological approximation takes place. Many of the older borrowings into Cantonese may have come through China Coast Pidgin. They are less clumsy by and large, and often take account of stress in an interesting fashion. Cheung (1969) has remarked that there is a clear tendency for English borrowings in Cantonese (derived from speech) to be assigned a high tone on the stressed syllable.

Compare these examples from MIX. They are transcribed using the IPA (1970) system: Symbols should be taken as having their Cantonese values, if they are part of the Cantonese phonological system.

MIX word	Origin (stress marked)
[ˊmai –k'rou]	mícro
[˥p'aːt˥ˎt'iː]	párty
[ˌa: ˥fɛi]	affí(liated)
[˷p'ou ˥lit˥]	polít(ical)

In these examples, and consistently throughout the tape-recordings with few exceptions, English stress is transmuted into high tone in well assimilated words. This can be seen with particular force in these examples:

| [˷t'ju ˥t'ɔː] | tutórial |
| [˥t'ju ˷t'aː] | tútor |

Here two phonologically very similar words have different stress patterning, and corresponding different tonal structure. What possible explanation is there for these correspondences between high tone and stress?

Until the mid-1950's it was widely accepted (see Bolinger, 1958) that the principal characteristic of and cue to stress was loudness. However, Fry (1958) demonstrated that pitch is a better cue to stress than loudness or duration. Bolinger (1958) also performed experiments which showed that "pitch is our main cue to stress" (p. 111), and "speakers . . . instinctively look for correlations of HIGH pitch and stress" (p. 133).

Since high pitch is an overwhelmingly important clue to stress, it seems perfectly natural that native speakers of a tone language such as Cantonese should, in borrowings, treat stress as tone. Additional evidence for this conclusion is that speakers of Nigerian tone languages who admix English lexis also engage in "replacement of stress features with tone" (Agheyisi, 1977: 107).

Grammar

This section is a tentative description of the grammatical composition of MIX. There will be an initial account of its surface characteristics, and then an attempt to derive principles which account for some of the systematicity in the mixing process. It is possible that these principles are generalizable to some of the other mixtures of codes referred to in the introduction to this chapter. Finally some of the elements unique to MIX will be described.

The transcription which is used here is the well known Yale system for Cantonese, and normal orthography for English: the English elements are also underlined to aid in their identification. Approximate translations are given below in brackets.

Readers unfamiliar with the grammar of Chinese may wish to know that Cantonese is an SVO language: determiners, adjectives and modifying nouns precede nouns; verbs are modified by auxiliary verbs and suffixes: and there are items that can behave in a similar way to English adverbs. In complex sentences there are major syntactic differences from English, for instance in relative constructions and topicalization.

The English elements found in MIX are mostly of one or two words in length, and are usually "content" or "open class" rather than "structure" or "closed class" words (see Quirk & Greenbaum, 1973: 19–20, for this distinction). The items are mostly English nouns, verbs and adjectives, with the occasional adverb. It can be seen from the description given in the preceding paragraph that such words can fit into the surrounding Cantonese phrase fairly easily, and there is little of the conflict of grammatical systems described in Pfaff (1979: 308–9, 315). Such conflict as does occur is described later.

Single words

The majority of English found in the recordings is in the form of single words surrounded by Cantonese. The following are examples:

nouns

kéuihdeih wah heui *barbecue*
(they say they're going to the barbecue)
heui *canteen* yám chàh
(let's go to the canteen for lunch)

néih *group* géi a?
(what group are you in?)

verbs

ngóh *take* sei fo
(I take four subjects)
ngóhdeih ho yi *adjust* ga *bubble* lo bo
(we can adjust the bubble!)
hóu doh yeh *press* néih
(literally: a lot of things press you,
i.e.: there are a lot of pressures on you)

adjectives

hóu *touching* a
(very touching!)
haih géi *depressing* ge, gó go *mood*
(it's quite depressing, that mood)
mātyeh haih hói sāam hóu chi *intimate* dī
(whatever is happy seems more intimate)
ngóh m̀h *sure*
(I'm not sure)

It is noticeable that English "structure" words such as determiners, conjunctions and auxiliary verbs almost never appear alone in the (predominantly Cantonese) discourse. There are, for example, no cases of an English determiner which does not qualify an English noun. Hence, while this occurred:

léuhng *part*
(two)

the type of structure exemplified by the following translation did not:

two ji
(parts)

The same appears to hold true for other mixed codes. For example, Pfaff (1979:292) has only three grammatical classes of single English words that are introduced into Spanish: nouns, verbs and adjectives. Timm (1975: 478–79) has a number of constraints that appear to act to produce a parallel effect. See also Poplack (1980: 602). Kachru's (1978: 39–41) constraints, numbers 5.2 – 5.4 on the mixing of Hindi and English reveal a similar situation. These writers also show that additive words cannot directly modify base language content words: for instance, in the case of MIX one does not find English adjectives preceding Cantonese nouns in the same noun phrase.

Single English lexical items are frequently totally assimilated into Cantonese grammar, hence in the previous example:

leúhng *part*
(two parts)

"part" lacks a plural "s" morpheme, as in Cantonese; in the case of

equip-jó
(has equipped)

an English verb has a Cantonese aspect marker. On occasions one finds English verbs or adjectives which have been repeated and/or divided in conformity with Cantonese syntax — for example:

neih *en* m̀h *enjoy* hái *choir*?
(do you enjoy yourself in the choir?)
de m̀h *desirable* a?
(is she desirable?)
o-mātyeh-*pen*?
(what do you mean, open?)

This behaviour is not frequent, and it produces effects that appear extraordinary to native English speakers.

Longer Elements

In the great majority of cases where the fragment of English consists of two words or more, it retains English grammar internally, while not disrupting the surrounding Cantonese grammar: that is, the fragment of English is fitted into the overall Cantonese syntax at the same point as the equivalent Cantonese element. The structure of the clause in Cantonese has some resemblances to English, so conflicts between the two systems in MIX are rare (see "Syntactic Conflicts" following). Examples of non-disruptive longer elements are:

m̀h sái joi wàn *part time job* a
(it's unnecessary to look for another part time job)

tēng dou dī *fellow student* wa *History* yáuh géi *topic*
(I hear that fellow students doing History have several topics)
haih m̀h haih seúng *train* yāt go *useful person* a?
(do they want to train a useful person?)

In the above examples it can also be seen that when two or more English
words are found together, they tend to be tightly linked by meaning. Some
longer segments of English are also found, for example:

leúhng go *group*, yāt go *group* jyúh góng yāt go
(two groups, one group starts discussing)
topic, the other group raised the question,
(a topic, the other group raised the question)
lìng ngoih yāt go *group answer the question.*
(the second group answer the question)

Here the use of determiners, and a past tense morpheme, mark these
stretches of English as retaining English grammar internally. Such longer
segments are usually used for special effects, such as humour or in the
above example as quotation from someone speaking in English. An
example of humorous effects in using longer stretches of English is the
following, in which a student who arrived late was offered a chair with
exaggerated formal politeness (with shouts of laughter from on-lookers):

Speaker A: After you ... I am glad to sit on it, but you're the first one.
                 Come on now.
Speaker B: Enjoy your privilege ...

This use of longer stretches of English for special effect is discussed at
greater length in the next chapter (it is "rhetorical code-switching" rather
than "code mixing" as defined in the introduction to Chapter 4).

Also found on tape were expressions such as:

man and society
let bygones be bygones
first come first served.

These appear to be idioms transferred intact from English; similarly Pfaff
(1979: 296) mentions "the generally recognized possibility of borrowing
idiomatic phrases as units"; Poplack (1980: 586) also describes the phenomenon.

Syntactic Conflicts

In the tape-recorded conversations there are comparatively rare cases where the insertion of English influences the surrounding syntax. In the next quotation "leúih mihn" and "within" are approximate translation equivalents.

> hái yāt go *society* léuih mihn gám lēi
> (within one society like this)
> yāt go *society* haih *within* yāt go *country* wo
> (one society is within one country they say)

It can be observed that while "leúih mihn" is in its appropriate position in the Cantonese sentence structure (after the noun phrase), "within" precedes the noun phrases as in English syntactic structure. In other words the English lexical item has led to the adoption of an English syntactic structure. Another example is the following:

> néih ho yi *go and* tai hah
> (you can go and have a look)

In this structure in Cantonese there is no connective such as "and" to link the verbs. Nevertheless "*go*" and "tai" (see) are connected in this fashion here. A final example is:

> daaih bouh fahn *base* hái néih ge sìng jīk
> (a large part is based on your results)

In English "based" is followed by "on" in this construction. Cantonese, however, does not use such a prepositional verb structure. Nevertheless, in this utterance the verb "base" is followed by the Cantonese locative "hái", which violates the syntax of Cantonese. I have also heard "*depend* hái". This type of syntactic conflict is uncommon.

Underlying Regularities in Syntactic Mixing

This survey of MIX grammar is brief — a more detailed analysis can be found in Gibbons (1979b). It is sufficient, however, to exemplify the underlying patterning in the pentration of English into Cantonese. It was observed that the English elements in MIX are never "structure" words standing alone although structure words are found in conjunction with "open class" words, and the same appears to hold true for the data in Pfaff (1979), Kachru (1978) and Timm (1975). In attempting to account for this regularity, a surface grammar of the non-transformational phrase structure/constituent type will be used. Although no claims are made for the theoretical validity of this type of grammar, it has proved useful in the analysis of natural discourse, particularly in psycholinguistics (see for example the review of research in Clark & Clark, 1977: 43–54).

If the utterances on the tapes are analysed in this way, then in virtually all the thousands of examples where a single word of English occurs, that word is innermost in the sense that it is immediately enclosed by a pair of brackets: for example:

((ngóh) (*take*) (sei (fo)))
I take four subjects

(((bīn) (yāt(go (kwok gā))))   ((*start*)   (nī (dī(*revolution*))) a)?
which   country   started   these   revolutions?

((ngóhdeih) (hó yíh (*adjust*))(ga (*bubble*)))
we   can   adjust   the bubble

((nī douh) ((*contract*) gán) (gó (dī (*muscle*))))
hóra   are contracting   thóse muscles

Where two or more words of English are introduced, one will be the innermost in the phrase, while the other will be the next innermost. For example:

(((séung (*train*)) (yāt(go (*useful* (*person*)))) a)
they want to train a   useful person
(((giu) ngóh)   ((*explain*) (*the (reason)*)))
asking me to   explain the reason
(gó (go (*Arts* (*student*)))) (dōu) (haih (*St. (John's)*)))
that Arts student   also is from St. John's

This mixing process can therefore be summarized in a comparatively simple way:

"Intrusion of code A into base code B takes place at the innermost parts of the syntactic structure."
(The use of the plural "parts" allows for next innermost position of other elements.)

This rule summarizes in an economical fashion most of Kachru's (1978: 39–40) constraints, *viz*:

"*5.2 Conjunction Constraint*
In the code mixing of South Asian languages the English conjunctions *and*, *or*, etc., are not used to conjoin non-English NP's or VP's."
"*5.3 Determiner Constraint*
There are several constraints on the items which can be code-mixed in a noun phrase in pre-head position."
(Kachru exemplifies with numerals and demonstratives)
"*5.4 Complementizer Constraint*
There are some constraints on code-mixing in complementizers. Consider the following:
(a) if the two sentences are from the same source languages, a complementizer from another source is not inserted."

However, this simple rule does not cover all Kachru's constraints, so it might require some modification to cover his data.

As already noted, Pfaff (1979) says that "single lexical item" switches are all Nouns, Verbs or Adjectives, so this rule may explain some of the phenomena she describes. It appears to work for nearly all the examples she provides.

It is, of course, impossible to say that this rule is generalizable to all admixture into a base code, but it may prove to be a step towards a (probably more abstract) universal rule.

Antonomous Elements

As in areas of phonology and lexis, there are certain elements which could be said to be unique to the mixed code. They are few in number, and include the following:

(a) *Expressions of percentage.*

In the mixed language these are regularly expressed as in the two examples below:

> yih sahp go *percent*
> (twenty (classifier) percent)
> luhk sahp go *percent*
> (sixty (classifier) percent)

As the numbers are in Cantonese, this is not an internally structured fragment of English: the addition of the classifier "go" means that it is not a literal translation of an English sentence. However, the Cantonese equivalents are:

> baak fahn jī yih sahp
> (literally: from a hundred parts twenty)
> baak fahn jī luhk sahp
> (literally: from a hundred parts sixty)

The mixed expressions of percentage are clearly not Cantonese, although there is a cognate Cantonese expression which cannot be used for percentages. The expression of percentage is therefore neither English nor Cantonese, and can only be seen as separate, possibly an extension of English or Cantonese.

(b) *Cardinal number questions*

For example:

> A: néih *group* géi a?
> (literally: your group which? i.e. which group are you (in)?)
> B: *group ten*

In response to the question, the statement form is "group" plus cardinal number. The question form reflects this, because the Cantonese question word for cardinal number "géi" (how many) is used. The equivalent Cantonese statement and question forms both require the use of ordinals. On the other hand, the question form is clearly not English. Here again then we have an instance of an autonomous syntactic structure.

(c) *Abbreviated idioms*

For example:

> cheuhng *choir*
> (literally: sing choir – i.e. sing in the/a choir)

The constructions used in both English and Cantonese are "sing *in* (a)choir", so this is part of neither language.

There are probably other syntactic structures of this type, but the researcher is not part of the bilingual speech community, and its members are rarely aware of this type of behaviour, so the detection of such forms is problematic.

Lexis

Pfaff (1979) in her study of the speech of Chicanos (Mexican Americans) pointed out that English words could be assimilated in varying degrees. Words that were consciously introduced as "foreign" to the surrounding discourse were often marked as such. She writes (p. 297) "there are often cues in the utterances themselves which indicate the speaker's perception of the foreignness of a word. Cues ... include hesitation, asides, and translation or paraphrase." Such words were also largely unassimilated to surrounding phonological and grammatical systems. At the other pole, there were some words such as "taipiar" (to type) which were phonetically and grammatically assimilated. Pfaff also writes, however, that "the categories are inherently squishy rather than discrete" (p. 296), and she points out that some words that were comparatively unassimilated in form were still "not foreign". The situation in the student speech community is broadly similar. There are conscious borrowings from English, of the type referred to earlier as intra-sentential code-switching. These are often marked by hesitation, a slowing in pace, and a general impression of "spoken inverted commas". There is also a class of English words which are used naturally as part of student discourse, but are relatively unassimilated in form (see below). Finally, there is a group of well assimilated lexical items which are, as we have already noted, highly integrated to a phonological system which is predominantly Cantonese. Intra-sentential code-switching is dealt with in the next chapter, so here we will examine the latter two groups of items that are in regular use in student speech. However, it should be noted at this point that, as in Pfaff's data, the boundaries between these types of lexis are "squishy", in fact they may not comprise distinct classes at all, but some form of continuum. Nevertheless, this classification aids greatly in the description.

Less Integrated Words

Examples: (medical students) kidney, enzyme, bilateral, function, blind spot, maxima, patient, diagnosis.
(sociology students) polarise, revolution, equality, under-developed, materialistic.
(geography students) systems approach, plane.
(philosophy students) valid, logic, premise.

These terms are, by and large, specialist terms from the student's academic area. There is a tendency for these words not to be highly assimilated to Cantonese systems, retaining many English features. Kwok Chan & Sun (1972: 76) may have this form of behaviour in mind when they write of

University students speaking "Chinglish", which consists of "Chinese laced with occasional English terms". I have heard many other speakers express the view that MIX is Cantonese, with a few extra technical terms from English where Cantonese equivalents are unfamiliar or non-existent. Two major assumptions underlie this view: first concerning the nature of MIX (it is Cantonese) and second the motivation or "triggering" of the introduction of English elements (due to lack of availability of Cantonese). These assumptions will be examined later.

There appears to be fairly consistent semantic modifiction in the use of many of these terms. Although students were aware of a potential range of meanings when questioned, in their tape recorded speech such terms are used largely when the topic is academic, and with a specialist meaning. Examples are:

blind spot – used only for an insensitive area of the retina, not "a failure in understanding".

"arts"   – used only to mean Arts Faculty (many times), never "the arts", i.e. cultural activity.

This narrowing to a single domain is found quite consistently throughout the recordings.

Well Assimilated Words

Examples:

Form (square brackets assumed)	Source	Meaning
SOCIAL LIFE		
–fit^l ´wui	(Fr.) fête + (Cant) /´wui/ (meeting)	a party
ˋsou –kɛt^l	so. gat.	social gathering
¯p at^l t´i	party	as source
¯stɛˊti	steady	a "steady" (boyfriend or girl friend)
spɔt k´ɛp^l (hall of residence)	sports captain	as source
¯rɛˊsi	resident	a resident member of hall of residence
–a: ¯fei	affil. (?)	an affiliated member of hall of residence
–hɔ	hall	hall of residence
¯ju -hɔ	U. Hall (?)	University Hall
¯wo: ˏtɛn	Warden	as source

POLITICAL LIFE

_noŋ _k'ɔn	no confidence	(take a) vote of no confidence
⁻ts'ɛ'lou	chair + (Cant.)	Chairman
	/ˈlou/ (guy)	
_a: ⁻keins	against	oppose
⁻p'ou´si	post	post in a society
sou k'ɔn	So. Con. (?)	social convenor
sɛk¹	sec. (?)	secretary

CAMPUS GEOGRAPHY
AND INSTRUCTIONS

ju –kei	U. (?) + (Cant.) /–kei/ (money-making establishment)	(H.K.) University (with cynical connotations of financial reasons for a degree)
⁻la:i –kei	library + (Cant.) /–kei/	library
_ri ⁻sœ f	reserve	reserve book room
⁻nou´si	Knowles	Knowles Building
⁻k'ɛn ⁻t'in	canteen	as source
⁻lɔk¹ˊ k'a:	locker	as source

COMMON ACADEMIC

_t'ju⁻t'ɔ:	tutorial	as source
⁻tap¹ –pu	double	duplicate copy of a book
⁻ɛ´sei	essay	as source
⁻k'ɔm –p'ou	compo.	composition (essay)
⁻k'ap¹ˊ fa:	cover	cover academic material
ˇfeilou	fail (also Cant. "fat guy")	to fail
⁻tsɔk¹ _ka:	geography	(academic study of) geography
sou wœk¹	social work	(academic study of) social work
_sai ⁻k'ou	psycho (?)	(academic study of) psychology

ATTITUDES

ˇfu ⁻luk¹	fluke	adj. or noun — person who got through with the minimum of work
–fat¹ˊsi	fussy	adj. similar to "frivolous"
–sɔ´fu	soft	adj. easy, or soft as in "soft option", usually in "a 'soft' course"

This is a substantial sample of well integrated lexis, sufficient for the purposes of this description. There are many other words of this type. Certain characteristics of these words are immediately apparent. Firstly, unlike the subject specific academic jargon described above, this lexis is usually concerned with matters common to most students — it might be said to refer to *student life*. This includes student politics, beliefs and attitudes, social life, campus geography and institutions, and common academic names (e.g. subject names, and words such as "lecturer", "tutorial").

Another major characteristic is, in most cases, a considerable divergence from the source word. This usually involves changes in form, and sometimes also in meaning. If we look first at form, most well-integrated terms conform to the preference in Chinese for words of one or two syllables — see Chung (1975). This has resulted in some major changes in the form of the word. A second formal characteristic is the presence of tone in most cases, with the relation to stress discussed earlier. A third formal feature is the far-reaching accommodation to the MIX phonological system discussed previously. There are also some loan blends such as [–fit¹ ẃui] and [⁻la:i –kei]. The combined effect of these various processes has resulted in forms which differ radically from their source, to the point of being virtually unrecognizable in some instances.

In meaning, too, a number of these terms have undergone extensive modification. Perhaps the most interesting in this respect are the last group, particularly [ˌfu⁻luk¹] and [–fat¹ ˊsi]. I have examined the meaning of these words in interview, and also by a word association test. They reflect resistance to a prevailing student ethic of diligence, sometimes taken to the point of massive rote learning – Fu (1975: 90–91) describes as typical "rote learning and passivity, strong incentives to study, great powers of persistence, a reluctance to criticise . . .". By contrast, informants state that [ˌfu⁻luk¹] is used to describe a student who gets through University with a degree, while doing the least work possible. In the process, the abstract noun "fluke" meaning "a lucky incident" has become an adjective or animate noun. [–fat¹ ˊsi] usually refers to the type of student that is interested in social life rather than study: it is often used to mean "not serious", hence the equivalent "frivolous". A recent poster on campus advertising "fussy games" baffled expatriate staff. Again this term has diverged far from its original meaning ("attentive to detail"). Many of the other items listed above have become specialized in meaning, although not as radically as (ˌfu⁻luk¹). For instance, in English the term "hall" has a fairly extensive semantic range, including the entrance corridor of a building (as in "hall stand"), and large buildings for public performances (e.g. "Concert Hall"). In the recordings, the term [–hɔ] is reserved for "halls of residence", in particular halls of residence of the University of Hong Kong.

The lexical items that have undergone these changes have become to some extent distinctive. In form, and in some cases meaning, they have moved away from their English source. Indeed, many of them are unintelligible to native speakers. In addition, the student speech community does not treat them as "foreign". They are a fully integrated part of normal student discourse in a similar way to certain English words used by Nigerians (Agheyisi, 1977: 105). On the other hand they are not Cantonese: they have not been accepted into the wider Cantonese speech community, and they have been modified to conform to systems that are not entirely Cantonese (for instance [⁻stɛ 'ti] retains initial [#st–] and [–ri ⁻sœf] has a final [–f#] – both unacceptable in the Cantonese phonological system). As a test, the intelligibility of various of these items was checked with Cantonese-English bilinguals teaching at Jinan University, Guangzhou. They found them unintelligible, even though some of the subjects graduated from the University of Hong Kong some decades previously. A sentence taken from one of the tapes which contains a number of well integrated words was also unintelligible:

/ˈnei/ [ˌaːˈfei] /–aː/ [⁻rɛ ˈsi ⁻ou ⁻hɔ] /–a/
(are you an affiliated member or a resident member of Old Halls?)

So some of these elements cannot be understood by people who speak both English and Cantonese, and consequently there is a sense in which these words can be said to belong neither to English nor to Cantonese, and thus to have a degree of autonomy.

A Word Association Experiment

In this experiment students from the Faculties of Arts, Social Science and Science at the University of Hong Kong were asked to write down the first word that came to mind when they heard stimulus words (after eight initial dummy items to allow the subjects to become accustomed to the situation and task). The stimulus words were English, Cantonese and well-assimilated words of the type just discussed. A number of these were translation equivalents.

When the responses were examined, the stimulus words had in most cases produced responses in three "milieux". The responses to English words were mostly concerned with activities connected with academic study: the responses to well-integrated words were largely concerned with students' social life within their peer group: Cantonese words evoked responses mainly concerned with life outside the educational sphere, predominantly associated with behaviour rooted in Chinese traditions, and centred on family life. These responses could not be attributed to the content of the words chosen, since some were translation equivalents of other test items.

This experiment supports the description of semantic specialization given above. This process has been found in other situations where admixture has occurred. For example, the English element in modern Amharic is limited to certain domains such as machinery, and such lexis has lost other potential meanings. Cooper (1969) has performed a similar experiment, in which word associations were linked, in his terminology, to specific domains.

MIX – Classification and Speculations

We have seen in this chapter that admixture appears to take two forms. One is intra-sentential code-switching, in which the English element in introduced quite consciously as a communication strategy. Other English elements, however, have become more integrated into MIX, and comprise sub-systems which are no longer English yet are not Cantonese. This process has been found at segmental, supra-segmental, grammatical, lexical and semantic levels.

This leaves the problem of classifying MIX, inasmuch as it is Cantonese augmented with elements of English and other elements or subsystems that are not entirely English or Cantonese. Clearly simple borrowing cannot account for the semantic changes we have observed, nor for the existence of idiosyncratic formal elements belonging neither to L1 nor to L2: furthermore, borrowing typically requires only a monolingual competence. The first point holds true for theories of *interference*, and furthermore interference normally carries with it the idea of errors in L1, L2, or both; although there are a few fossilized English language errors to be found in MIX, the main point is that it has independent norms. Indeed, Ma & Herasimchuk (1971: 351–53) attack the adequacy of interference as a means of describing intra-group (rather than intergroup) bilingualism. *Code-switching* similarly will not account for the autonomous element. *Pidgins* are codes which have been developed as a form of basic communication between groups who do not share a common language; a pidgin is an "auxiliary contact language" (DeCamp, 1971: 16); MIX by contrast has developed within a single group and is used only for intra-group communication. *Creoles* are normally regarded as having developed from pidgins, so this term is also inappropriate. However, the English element in MIX has many of the characteristics of creoles. Hymes (1971b: 75–76) gives these properties as typical of creoles: convergence, "mingling, coalescence, even fusion of two varieties", expansion, autonomy, native speakers, and semantic specialization. Looking at these in turn, *convergence* is defined by Hymes (1971b) as "approximation of one variety to another"; the English element in MIX has in many instances approximated to Cantonese, sometimes to the point where some English elements have "mingled" and coalesced with Cantonese. There has been a small amount of *expansion* to enable expression of specific student attitudes. As we have seen, MIX has developed *autonomous* elements at a number of linguistic levels. I have heard tape recordings of the speech of the young children of post-graduates who are evidently growing up speaking a mixture of English and Cantonese similar to MIX, comprising a potential *native speaker* population. Finally, we have seen that *semantic specialization* of lexis is a clearly marked feature of MIX. Yet MIX is not a creole: it has not developed from a pidgin, and as these processes have taken place almost exclusively within the small English component, they have had far less influence overall than they would in the case of a true creole. MIX also differs from Platt's (1975) *creoloid* in that it has not emerged as a result of the standard contact situation between two groups, but rather within a single group as a result of the contact of two cultures: in consequence it fails to meet one of Platt's criteria (Table E2, p. 372) "used as a *lingua franca* in the wider speech community". Platt also states that the transfer of features should be "from the languages of several (sometimes unrelated) ethnic groups"; in MIX, of course, there is only one source of extra features. These differences spring from a major underlying dissimilarity: Platt is thinking of a superordinate language of inter-ethnic communication, affected by substrata of other first languages, whereas MIX is an ethnic native language influenced by a superordinate language — almost a creoloid in reverse.

What we are in fact looking for, then, is a process which has much in common with creolization, but which does not have a pidgin as a starting point. Hymes (1971b: 78–79) uses the term "koinéizing" to describe exactly this kind of process. He remarks that, in both creoles and koinés (pp. 78–79): "Expansion in content, admixture, and expansion in role as a primary language are found."

As we have seen, MIX has an expanded vocabulary, plentiful admixture, and among bilinguals has taken over the role of pure English, which among earlier generations of students was used to discuss academic topics.

In using the term "koinéizing" to refer to the fusion of languages, Hymes is extending its meaning, since it referred originally to a fusion of dialects (see for example Nida & Fehderau, 1970, and Dillard, 1972). The original koiné was the standard Greek language derived from a number of Greek dialects; Dillard (1972) in fact defines koinéizing as a "dialect levelling". However, the boundary between a dialect and a language is one that has been closely questioned in recent times, and many linguists would now say that the distinction is socio-political rather than linguistic. Distantly related languages, for example, are sometimes called "dialects" in China, while the Scandinavian languages might well be called dialects in another socio-political situation, since they are mutually intelligible. Blanc (1968) first extended the use of the term koiné when he referred as such to modern Hebrew, which has fused different earlier forms of the language with elements from European languages particularly Yiddish and English. Hymes (1971b) in turn pointed out that there are strong resemblances between the processes that modern Hebrew has undergone, and the development of English under the impact of French and Latin after the Norman conquest. Hebrew and English are both standard languages, of course, but Dillard (1972) points out that the product of koinéizing need not necessarily be a standard language.

If we therefore accept Hymes' and Blanc's use of the term koinéizing, it probably constitutes the best description of the process that MIX is undergoing. The parallels between Modern Hebrew, post-Norman-conquest English and MIX are very striking. The situations which gave birth to all three are similar. All have expanded their function to cover new areas. Hebrew, for centuries a liturgical and literary language, had suddenly to expand dramatically to become the national language of a state that was struggling to modernize very rapidly. Hymes (1971b: 79) writes of English: "after the Norman conquest English was subordinate, limited in function. It subsequently expanded in function, replacing French (in the law courts for instance) and replacing, or rivalling, Latin, too." Cantonese is effectively subordinate in function to English in Hong Kong, and in Hong Kong the pressure to modernize and Westernize is strong. In MIX the new areas are primarily student life, or else are specialized and academic, and Western in origin (as is often the case with European elements in Hebrew).

As a sociolinguist might predict, the language forms which resulted from similar social situations have much in common. In all three cases the original local language remains systemically dominant, but the systems which have emerged show influences from other languages at most linguistic levels, and also have unique features which differ from any of the sources. We have already seen this in MIX, and Blanc mentions European influences in the semantics and phonology of modern Hebrew, and shows how a new phonological system has emerged. He remarks (p. 247) "the 'emergent standard' . . . is . . . strongly marked by the dominant European substrata and adstrata in grammar and vocabulary". English similarly has composite systems at various linguistic levels; in phonology, for example, the Germanic fortis-lenis distinction was extended to include a /f–v/ contrast. At the grammatical level English has developed away from both its Romance and Germanic forebears, in that it depends more heavily than either of them on word order rather than morphology — a pidgin-like development that may possibly be the result of the contact situation. English also shows differentiation of semantic field in lexis, which we discussed as typical of MIX: perhaps the best known instance is the use of Germanic items for food animals, and equivalent items of French origin to refer to meats only.

These resemblances constitute a strong case for describing the process which MIX is undergoing as koinéizing. However, MIX should not be regarded as a koiné, since it has not stabilized sufficiently yet, nor has the process gone as far as in the case of English or Hebrew. Nevertheless it is possible that a full koiné may emerge in time in Hong Kong, taking into account first that some children of the educated élite are growing up speaking a mixture of English and Cantonese: second that the educated élite played an important role in the changes which led to the formation of modern Hebrew and English; and third, that more than 87% of Hong Kong's secondary schools are English medium, and as universal secondary education has been introduced, so the contact situation is becoming a widespread experience. MIX may therefore be an incipient koiné. (See the speculations in Chapter 7.)

The situation which gave birth to MIX — the use of a foreign language of instruction — is found in many other countries and appears to result in similar language phenomena. The writer has observed Arab students at the University of Madrid mixing Spanish and Arabic; Indian students at British universities mixing Indian languages and English (see Setlur, 1973); African students mixing African languages and English at the University of Nairobi; Taiwanese medical students apparently also mix English and Mandarin; Blom & Gumperz (1972) have studied the mixing of Bokmål Norwegian standard and Ranamål dialect among Ranamål dialect-speaking university students and Agheyisi (1977) describes English "interlarding" in the speech of Nigerians, including university students. It seems highly probable that in other universities where the medium of instruction is other than the first language, similar forms of language behaviour have developed.

Outside the University context mention should be made of "the tongue of the Tirilones" or "Caló", spoken on the Mexican–American border and described by Coltharp (1965). There are many parallels with MIX. It is a language in part unintelligible to outsiders, predominantly Spanish but with a large English influence, especially at the lexical level, and it also has an idiosyncratic element. It has English influences at all levels in a similar way to MIX; in addition (Coltharp, 1965: 11) "contact with individuals of the dominant (Anglo) culture is slight". It is interesting to note that Caló is spoken mainly by people in the lowest stratum of society, in contrast to MIX which is used by a group of great prestige in the local society. The languages of other American immigrant communities have been well documented as going through a stage that appears to be koinéizing, but this is generally a step on the way to English monolingualism, or at least to a highly restricted role for the immigrant language. See, for example, Fishman, Cooper & Ma et al. (1971), Kartunnen (1976) and Diebold (1963).

As a result of changing world conditions, cultures are coming increasingly into contact. The pace of scientific and technological development is making necessary the acquisition and use of a language of wider communication for educational purposes. As the situation which gave rise to MIX becomes increasingly common it is likely that other such codes will appear.

Notes to Chapter 3

1. In the sections dealing with pronunciation the IPA (1949) phonetic symbols are used. The phonemic transcription of English follows Jones (1967).
2. Some English words are assigned tone in MIX. The IPA diacritics for Cantonese tone are the following (the high falling tone may be disappearing in Hong Kong).

   ⁻high level; ˋhigh falling; ˊhigh rising; –mid level;
   ₋low level; ˎlow falling; ˏlow rising.

4 An Ethnographic Approach

Introduction

Very typical of this approach is the ethnomethodology of writers such as Sacks, Schegloff and Jefferson. However, this book is concerned with code-mixing and code choice, and these writers do not in general concern themselves with such forms of variation.

Ethnographic studies of code choice are found in the work of researchers in the ethnography of speaking (notably Hymes and Gillian Sankoff), of Gumperz, of the Austin school and of scattered researchers elsewhere (see below). These writers share the common ethnographic approach of gathering substantial records of genuine situated speech, usually by participant observation, and then attempting to detect patterns using evidence internal to the data and the researcher's intuitions drawing on his/her social knowledge. Often patterning in code choice is explained by assigning social meaning to the choices. To a considerable extent the ethnographic approach consists of a methodology, so separate discussion of method and model will not be used here. Much of the work in code choice and code-mixing has been undertaken in the ethnographic tradition, so a review of some of this work can provide useful frameworks and contrastive information from other speech communities. The work of Gumperz to some extent bridges ethnographic, secular linguistic and macro-sociolinguistic approaches. In a number of well-known papers he has looked at style shifting, code-mixing and code-switching proper.

Blom & Gumperz (1972) use a mixture of ethnographic and semi-empirical approaches – "deductive reasoning supported by unstructured ethnographic observation" plus recordings of conversations in which the researchers manipulated the topic, selecting for analysis sections which appeared naturalistic. Blom & Gumperz make an important theoretical distinction between "situational switching" and "metaphorical switching". The first refers to the type of language behaviour discussed in Chapter 2 on the Sociology of Language, i.e. the participants, what is happening and the setting influence the code choice, and are also marked by it. As Blom & Gumperz (1972: 424) write, "The notion of situational switching assumes a direct relationship between language and social situation". By contrast "metaphorical switching" occurs when the code choices are not heavily constrained by the socio–situational context. The code choice then highlights an alternative social relationship between the participants; Blom & Gumperz write (1972: 425):

"Characteristically, the situations in question allow for the enactment of two or more different relationships among the same set of individuals. The choice of either (R) or (B) alludes to these relationships and thus generates meanings which are quite similar to those conveyed by the alternation between *ty* or *vy* in the examples from Russian literature cited by Friedrich (Chapter 9). We will use the term *metaphorical switching* for this phenomenon."

The *ty/vy* alternation marks the solidarity-status choice in personal relations (see also Brown & Gilman, 1960) – and it is clear from the article that (R) – the local dialect Ranamål – marks solidarity, while the use of the standard – (B) Bokmål – marks status. Blom & Gumperz speak of "code-switching" yet they also mention that for certain subjects the choices operate along continua and that there is substantial "mixing" rather than true code switching. The university students in their sample vary their speech along a cline, in the direction of the dialect or the standard. Blom & Gumperz (1972: 431) write:

"For the students, on the other hand, the distinction between dialect and standard is not so sharp ... their behaviour shows a range of variation rather than an alternation between distinct systems."

Blom & Gumperz do not give a name to this type of variation: in Chapter 5 of this book such behaviour is referred to as "code-swaying" in contrast to code-switching. References to, and influences from this article can be found in much subsequent work on code-switching and code-mixing.

Gumperz & Hernández-Chavez's (1971) study is based on unstructured recordings of Mexican–American conversations. The choices of English and Spanish are interpreted freely using internal evidence and native speaker intuition. The recordings contain extremely frequent code-switching within a single socio-situational context. These switches may take place within single sentences, or may involve idioms, but Gumperz & Hernández-Chavez, 1971: 319): "The greater part of the instances of true code-switching consist of entire sentences inserted into the other language text." Lexical insertion is also found, often a result of "difficulty in finding the right word" (p. 321). Among the motives for inter-sentential code-switching are quotation, emphasis, and topic — essentially rhetorical reasons. However, as with the Norwegian study discussed previously, the two languages are associated with different social values, Spanish with solidarity and English with status. Gumperz & Hernández-Chavez (1971: 327) make the important general point that "What the linguist sees merely as alternation between two systems, serves definite and clearly understandable communicative ends."

These two studies involving Gumperz have had considerable influence on subsequent Mexican-American studies. These latter are essentially ethnographic, and have gone further in attempting to distinguish types of switching, and rhetorical purposes for switching. Much of the work is associated with the University of Texas at Austin — Baker (1980) provides a useful survey, so there is little point in rehearsing this. Suffice to indicate briefly that the Austin school distinguish a number of levels of code-switching, including the situational type discussed in the sociology of language, and the metaphorical type discussed by Blom & Gumperz (1972) — see above. They have also found extensive use of English lexis in predominantly Spanish discourse — in this situation Spanish is referred to as the "base language". A number of motivations for code switches are described, including (Baker, 1980: 5, 13–16): "translations/explanations", "idioms", "repetitions", "quotations", "lexical gaps", "emphatic", "least effort principle", and "fullest expression". Many researchers into bilingual situations will find these categories immediately recognizable.

Another group of scholars, who might be loosely grouped as the "Commonweath school", consists of writers such as Annamalai (1971), Kachru (1978), Sridhar (1978), Agheyisi (1977) and Ure (1974). These writers have looked at "code-mixing", defined by Kachru (1978: 28) as follows:

> "The term 'code-mixing' refers to the use of one or more languages for consistent transfer of linguistic units from one language into another, and by such a language mixture developing a new restricted – or not so restricted – code of linguistic interaction."

The phenomena described by these writers appear to differ in type from those described by the Austin school. In the code mixtures described by the former, elements from a donor language are integrated into a base language to form a single composite code, with little awareness of code switching among speakers. A major motivation for this behaviour is that the donor language serves as an additive source of linguistic material in the development of specialized registers. Sridhar (1978: 115) writes:

"When a speaker wants to sound knowledgeable or authentic or simply wants to be precise in discoursing upon a specific topic, he tends to mix elements from the language commonly associated with that topic."

The prestige motive is also clearly present in this description.

In what has been written so far in this chapter we have seen that it is possible to categorize certain forms of code choice and code mixing, even though the categories are clearly not discrete. Indeed, given the complexity and lack of absolute rules in sociolinguistic behaviour one would expect overlap and occasionally conflict. Nevertheless these categories form a useful framework for description and permit the treatment of areas of bilingual behaviour in turn rather than as an undifferentiated whole. The three categories that will be used from now on are "situational code-switching","rhetorical code-switching" and "code mixing". Descriptions follow.

Situational Code-Switching

This is the type of language behaviour described in Chapter 2 under the "sociology of language". Choice of code within the speech repertoire is influenced by such socio-situational factors as physical context, what is happening, participants and topic. Interaction proceeds in a single code until one of these factors is changed. Such behaviour requires good control of a number of codes, and appears to be accessible to conscious introspection.

Rhetorical Code-Switching

The situational factors described above may leave open the possibility of using more than one code. In such a situation, speakers may exploit this possibility for rhetorical and social effects. This is the type of behaviour discussed by the Austin school and also by Gumperz & Hernández-Chavez (1971) and forms the focus of the next section of this chapter. Such code switching can take place when situational factors are held constant: consequently this behaviour is most common in groups which have some form of shared bilingualism — referred to by Ma & Herasimchuk (1971) as "intra-group bilingualism". Code switches of this type tend to take place at sentence or phrase boundaries. The "salting" of a discourse with elements from another code requires knowledge of the latter, but not necessarily high bilingual proficiency. Such code-switching may not always be entirely conscious, but its effects are often accessible to introspection.

Code-Mixing

This type of behaviour is described by the "Commonwealth" school, by McClure (1977) and by Blom & Gumperz (1972: 429–30). In this form of behaviour elements from one code become to some extent integrated into another. One code, the base code, is normally dominant, and speakers use the second code in an additive fashion. Elements from the latter code tend to be to some extent assimilated and consequently are used less consciously (Blom & Gumperz, 1972: 430). A code mixture is often felt to be a single code rather than rapid switching (see Elías-Olivares, 1979: 125; Ma & Herasimchuk, 1971: 359–60). Mixing can be distinguished from borrowing in that borrowings are used by monolinguals, while mixing is bilingual intragroup behaviour. Furthermore, borrowings tend to be totally assimilated to the receiving language, while mixed elements often systematically retain features of the donor language.

Applying the Ethnographic Approach

The data base for this study is that described in the introduction to Chapter 3. The approach will be used to analyse first rhetorical code-switching and then code-mixing. In the analysis of rhetorical code-switching the switch is treated as a meaning bearing part of the communication system. Rhetorical code-switching, in contrast to the situational type, often takes place within a sentence (it is intra-sentential) and may involve clauses, phrases or words inserted into a base language. In the description which follows, the switches are categorized by the rhetorical effect they produce.

Emphasis (see McClure & Wentz, 1975: 426; and Rayfield, 1970: 56)

A characteristic of both emphasis and clarification (see the following section) is "bilingual echoing" in which there is an immediate translation or near equivalent in the other language. This is exemplified by McClure & Wentz (1975) as follows:

yo soy segundo . . . . I'm second
(I'm second)

and by Rayfield (1970):

"she was a dream, *ir ken es kulen*, you can imagine"
(you can imagine)

Similar translations, presumably for emphasis, can be found in Ma & Herasimchuk (1971: 359):

Que son todos jovencitos, they're young
(they're all young)

and Gumperz & Hernández-Chavez (1971: 321) note " 'Si hay criaturas' . . . is directly translated without hesitation pause in the following sentence."

In the tape recordings of Hong Kong University students there are occasional examples of bilingual echoing, where emphasis is apparent in the pronunciation, for instance:

yáuh chāt, *seven*
(there are seven)

devote dī *time, devote* sìh gaan
(some) (time)

ngóh heui chīm jó meng a, ngóh *sign* jó la.
(I went and signed) (I signed)

Clarification (see McClure & Wentz, 1975: 427)

In what follows, clarification is conflated with McClure & Wentz's (1975) category "elaboration". In both cases an idea is expressed in two languages to make meaning clearer (although this bears some resemblance to "semantics" in the next section, here terms from both languages are used together). Examples from McClure & Wentz (1975: 427) are:

Roli, put that, *ahí ponla en el sacate, [hi] jito*
(there, put it on the grass, honey)
You(r) dog. *Tu perro!*
(Your dog)

Examples from the Hong Kong University students are:

hóu cheùhng sai, hóu *detail* gám duhk saai
(very detailed, very)   (thus to read it completely)

Speaker A: . . . tùhng hohk lúhk. B: *Record book* ga
(record book)   *(particle)*

and when two students were discussing a course:

géi hóu, j̄ik houh géi *interesting*
(quite good, that is quite)

On occasions an English word is subsequently translated or expanded in Cantonese, e.g.:

mouh ḡam níhn gám *simple*, gám gáan d̄an
(this year it's not so)   (so simple)

— in this case the Cantonese term augments the meaning of "simple".

Avoidance of Repetition

Another type of rhetorical device that uses translation is what appears to be the stylistic avoidance of repetition of a word by using its translation equivalent. This appears to be what is happening in the following examples (translation equivalents are starred thus *———* . . . *———*):

take d̄i *minor* ge *j̄ik waih*, m̀h hóu taai go
(some)   (posts, it's not a very
*important ge *post**

duhk māt yeh fo . . . *take* mātyeh fo
(which subjects do you take . . . which subjects do you take?)

Quotation

When something has been expressed initially in Code A, and is quoted later in a Code B context, it seems possible that it will be reported in the original code. This phenomenon has been noted by Elías-Olivares (1976: 208) who gives this example:

mi hija siempre me dice "When are you gonna get those pictures mom?"

(my daughter always says to me)

Rayfield (1970: 55) gives the following case of quotation:

I asked her: *"vus veynt ir?"*
(why are you crying?)

A surprisingly large proportion of the longer stretches of English in the student language data are of this type. In the following cases from different tapes, students are quoting tutors:

It doesn't matter, when the first time I do philosophy leh,
(particle)

I met the same problem with you ga, kéuih wa néih *by the*
(he says, you)

time of May leh, *you'll understand what it means* ga laak. Cheh!
(particle)   (particles) (Rot!)

(this example is interesting in the lack of accuracy in the quotation, and the addition of Cantonese "utterance particles" (Gibbons, 1980) to English sentences)

haih a, *in writing or come and see* kéuih
(yes)   (him)

lihng ngōi yāt go *group answer the question*
(the other)

To conclude this section on rhetorical strategies, one should perhaps point out that this use of English is far outweighed by the introduction of single lexical items, which appear integrated into the discourse, rather than introduced for effect.

Semantically Motivated Introduction of Single Words

The title of this section refers to the tendency for bilinguals to use the full range of their lexical repertoire (from whatever language) to express precisely and concisely a desired meaning. On some occasions this may result from a gap in the bilingual's knowledge of one of his/her languages: on other occasions the characteristics of the semantic structure of the languages themselves may be involved. Presumably this form of behaviour began as conscious code-switching to facilitate the expression of the desired meaning: however, in time, if words are used frequently enough they become part of the normal unconscious form of speech. It is in this category therefore that we find a number of items whose status as either rhetorical code-switches or code-mixing is unclear.

Limited Access to Terms

I have already remarked on the prevailing view that English academic terms are not accessible to students in Cantonese. This appears to be what Elías-Olivares (1976: 183–86) calls *limited access to terms*. She believes that some Chicanos lack Spanish technical terms because they have received their schooling in English — an almost exact parallel with students at the University of Hong Kong. She was challenged by Huerta (1978: 47) who found that most Chicano bilinguals in fact do know the Spanish equivalents of such technical terms. This observation is supported by Rayfield's (1970) work with Yiddish speakers in America. She too was intrigued by the use of English lexis in predominantly Yiddish discourse, so she noted the English terms and tested the speakers to discover whether they knew the Yiddish equivalents: in nearly all cases they did. She writes (p. 50):

> "In most cases, however, there is no obvious reason for the use of a loanword; most of the loanwords have well-known equivalents in Yiddish.
>
> This fact was brought out by the Recollection Test. The words on this test were selected on the grounds that (1) they are very commonly used by the *bilingual majority*, and (2) they might be expected to have equivalents in European Yiddish. All the informants, except the few who had learned their Yiddish in America, scored high on the Recollection Test, *i.e.* they could recall without much difficulty, even out of context, the Yiddish equivalents of the English loanwords they used every day. But they still used the loanwords almost exclusively."

In the case of Hong Kong students, it is most unlikely that they did not know the Cantonese equivalents of words such as these (which they produced in English): country, desire, English, fight, free, group, against, the best, Cantonese, Chinese (!), like, singing, problem, world. A number of English terms had Cantonese equivalents in the same discourse, e.g.

take, patient, ferry, Chinese History, course, holiday, Athens. Although the Cantonese terms may not be the first that come to mind, it is comparatively rare to find in the corpus English lexical items whose Cantonese equivalents are not known. The *limited access* theory therefore explains only a small proportion of the use of English terms.

Apposite Terms

Here, rather than referring to gaps in the bilingual's knowledge of his languages, we are discussing a bilingual making full use of the expressive potential of his or her verbal repertoire. It is widely accepted that the lexis and idioms of one particular language rarely correspond exactly with those of another. Although translation equivalents may overlap, it is unusual to find words in two languages (especially non-cognate languages) that cover exactly the same area of meaning, and which have identical connotation and collocation. When bilinguals are conversing, it would not be unexpected if they were to use lexis or idioms from more than one code, if this enabled them to express their meanings more precisely and concisely (given, of course, the absence of a strong social rule against such behaviour). This occurs in Spanish–American code-mixing, for example Wentz (1977) describes "the inclusion of elements of one code in a sentence or constituent of another code used principally for the expression of a more apposite unit". Huerta (1978) makes a similar point. This interpretation is convincing when applied to the words listed under "attitudes" in Chapter 3. These English words have been modified to enable students to express clearly current attitudes to student life (this type of expansion in a code is often mentioned in creole studies – see Hymes, 1971a: 78–79). Other examples in the data were clearly of intra-sentential code–switching type — the items were marked by hesitation, etc. One example was the English word "friendly": there is no single Cantonese item which exactly encapsulates the meaning of this word, and student bilinguals affirm that this is why the English word is used. Such an explanation probably does not apply to English technical terms, however, since these normally have equivalents in the technical lexicon of other languages, including Chinese.

Repetition

A related phenomenon may be those cases where one speaker uses an English term, and the following speaker accepts that specification of content, and continues to use the same term. Huerta (1978: 38) mentions this phenomenon and calls it *repetition*. It is difficult to identify examples in student speech, since both the specialized academic lexis and well-integrated words are sufficiently common for it to be tendentious to classify them as repetitions rather than normal usage. (However, it does seem possible that the group of speakers determines by some form of consensus the amount of English lexis used – see Chapter 5.) On occasions the students use English for rhetorical effects, and on these occasions if a fellow student continues with the English term, it is probably a case of repetition. One clearly marked example was found on a tape where the English word "go" was used on a number of occasions. Normally the Cantonese 'heui' is used; in fact "go" did not occur on any other recording, nor has the writer heard it on campus. In this recording Speaker B uses the term frequently, probably to push his point after some prevarication by Speaker B. Speaker A in his first utterance *also* uses "go" and then proceeds to use "heui " ("go" and "heui" are italicized in the transcript to facilitate comparison).

B: dōu haih *no go* a. *go* m̀h *go* a néih?
(it's best no(t) to go. Are you going?)
nám chìng chó meih a? *go* jauh *go*,
(have you thought it out? If you're going then)
m̀h *go* jauh m̀h *go* la.
(go, if not, then don't).
A: m̀h *go* a. hóu síu yáuh *heui* ge wa!
(I'm not going. Very few say they're going.)
m̀h haih sihng yaht *heui* ge wo.
(They're not going for the whole day, they say.)

It seems fairly likely in this example that A uses "go" because B does so. Repetition explains only a small number of cases of use of English, however.

Idioms

Another case where the exact meaning of one language is hard to capture in another is in the area of *idioms*. Other writers have noted the introduction of idioms from the second language into the base language, for example Pfaff (1979: 296), Huerta (1978: 38), Poplack (1980: 586) and Clyne (1967: 41). There are a number of examples in student conversation, such as "let bygones be bygones", "first come first served": on one occasion an English idiom is translated word for word "yih laih yih heui" (easy come easy go). Set phrases are also found, e.g. "man and society", "data processing".

Taboos

A final example of students making use of the expressive capability of both languages at their disposal is in the area of taboo words and topics. Since the vocabulary of a foreign or second language rarely carries the same emotional force as native words, it is not uncommon to find taboo words translated into a foreign language; evidence the educated English use of Latin words for sexual organs, a close parallel to the use of English itself as a technical language in many other societies. Rayfield (1970: 57) mentions this in her Yiddish community, and educated Indians have informed the writer that they use English for taboo meanings. Although the Hong Kong University students (understandably) did not record discussions of taboo subjects, reliable informants state that they do use English lexis in this way, and Luke & Richards (1982) also document this in Hong Kong.

There is evidence, therefore, that in a limited number of cases one motive for the insertion of English is semantic in nature, i.e. it facilitates the more precise expression of desired meaning or carries a more appropriate connotation. It should be noted, however, that technical terms do not fall happily into this category and many of the lexical items describing campus life have clear and accessible Cantonese alternatives. The motivation therefore explains a small proportion of the use of English elements, but leaves most unexplained. Rhetorical strategies similarly leave unexplained the motivation for the additional systematic elements from English, and the use of most of the terms, both well integrated and less integrated, discussed earlier. It is nonetheless interesting to note the similarities between the semantic and rhetorical strategies of this speech community, and those of such disparate groups as Chicanos, German-Australians, Indians, and Yiddish-speaking Americans referred to in this discussion. Since much code choice behaviour remains unexplained by conscious communication strategies, possibilities in the domains of social and psychological causation will be examined in the remaining chapters.

Concept Formation

When Huerta (1978) and Elías-Olivares (1976) debate the reasons for the use of English rather than Spanish lexis in the domain of schooling, they do so in terms of the speakers' knowledge, or lack of knowledge of such vocabulary. This formulation may, however, be somewhat misleading. One part of the educational process itself is the development and labelling in the mind of the student of concepts and constructs. It is in the nature of education that many of these will be new to the student. It follows therefore that the *initial* concept formation and labelling takes place in the *language of education*: in the case of Chicanos, Nigerians (Agheyisi, 1977: 105) and Hong Kong students this language is often English. It also forms part of an interlocking framework of ideas received through the same medium. Subsequently the student may well come to associate the concept with terms in the mother tongue and other languages in his/her repertoire. Nevertheless, the English term is in some sense primary, and there would be no cause for surprise if this term came most readily to mind when the need arose to express a concept in the academic domain. In addition, the continuing use of English in education would tend to reinforce the English lexis, to the point where it is also the most *familiar* term for the concept. This provides a convincing explanation for the use of less integrated English academic lexis (see Chapter 4) by the Hong Kong University students, and is given some support by the results of the word association experiment described earlier. Nevertheless more empirical data are required before such a thesis can be advanced with any certainty. Ervin-Tripp (1967) in experiments with Japanese–American women found such an association between life experience and their two languages.

Identity Marking

Let us turn now to the well assimilated lexis (see Chapter 4) which refers largely to student life. As we have seen, this is a highly developed jargon, sometimes unintelligible to outsiders. Friendly & Glucksberg (1970: 65) discuss the acquisition of student slang (also often unintelligible to outsiders) at Princeton University in the following terms: "As an individual becomes a member of a group, the meanings of familiar words change, and new words are acquired" — the parallelism with MIX is striking. This they regard as a "socialisation process". Giles, Bourhis & Taylor (1977: 325–28) refer to large amounts of experimental evidence that speech is an important marker of social identity (perhaps the most important): in the words of Ross (1979: 5) language can "differentiate a collective we from an external they". Laver & Trudgill (1979: 3) also discuss the use in speech of "group markers" which reveal membership of a group, and "social markers" which "mark social characteristics such as regional affiliations, social status, educational status, occupation and social role". Applying this to the student speech community, one might speculate that the use of MIX, when it includes the well assimilated lexis, marks membership of the student speech community. To fellow students this might serve as a "group marker", indicating solidarity; to outsiders it might serve as a "social marker" indicating social and educational status. These possibilities are explored in the matched guise experiment reported in Chapter 6.

Evaluating the Ethnographic Approach

The use of the ethnographic approach here raises many of the issues implicit in research performed in this manner. With regard to data *collection* the advantages of working with natural language behaviour (influenced as little as possible by the researcher) appear obvious. Our objective is after all to discover how people behave in real life in their community. The best source of primary data is therefore the direct recording of behaviour in these circumstances. This type of research may reveal delicate or covert areas that need to be probed using other approaches.

Problems can arise with data *analysis*, however. The use of introspection and internal evidence is an almost inevitable first step in virtually any form of scientific endeavour. However, if the "rhetorical code-switching" section is examined, it becomes clear that the strategies are defined by examples, and the examples are placed within strategies — a fundamentally tautological procedure. Furthermore, the lack of concrete objective criteria can result in imprecise or complex categories. Questionable categorization can be found in much of the work discussed at the beginning of this chapter — evidence the fact that Baker's (1980) survey is subtitled "untangling the terminology".

Since ethnographic data analysis is essentially discursive there are no quantifiable empirical data as evidence of correspondence between linguistic and social elements. Some scholars, including myself, regard this as a weakness (see for example Coulthard, 1977: 91): others, especially ethnomethodologists, view it as a strength (see Turner, 1974: 8–81). Indeed, it is unwise to place too much reliance upon numerical analysis. Most honest researchers would admit that it is possible to manipulate figures to produce desired outcomes, and it is not uncommon for findings which conflict to be quietly ignored. However, numerical data analysis does permit replication and the resolution of conflicts over interpretations of data, while in many cases ethnographic analysis does not. Ethnographic analyses, because of their discursive nature, also render very difficult comparisons between different sets of data — in the case of sociolinguistics, comparisons between speech communities.

So on the one hand we have the necessity for and value of ethnographic studies; on the other the problems common to such studies. Perhaps the best solution is the one found in standard scientific methodology — to regard ethnographic studies as an essential hypothesis *generating* step in research, which then needs to be followed by more quantifiable (possible experimental) work, which can test in a replicable fashion previously generated interpretations of observed phenomena.

Next steps

Inasmuch as this work aims to achieve an understanding of the bilingual behaviour of a community, the preceding chapter has given some answers but has also thrown up a number of questions. In some speech communities (particularly the Spanish-American ones discussed previously) it appears that rhetorical code-switching explains much of the admixture of one language into another. However, this is not the case with the Hong Kong group studied here, where much of the admixture is of the unconscious code-mixing type discussed by the Commonwealth school. I have suggested that some of this code-mixing is a result of concept development taking place in the second language (English) and that some form of identity and status marking may be involved. Both of these suggestions require further investigation and support, and furthermore much of the code-mixing behaviour needs further investigation since it is still to some extent unexplained. It is to these issues that the next two chapters are addressed.

5 A Secular Linguistic Approach

Introduction

The term "secular linguistics" for this approach was proposed by Trudgill (1978: 11). It is also sometimes referred to as Labovian micro-sociolinguistics in honour of William Labov who has contributed so much to this area of knowledge. In this approach formality (elicited by changes in the situation) and sociodemographic factors (such as age, sex and social class) are related to linguistic variation — usually variation in speech sounds, but also in other elements such as grammatical morphemes. Labov (1972) provides the standard description. A major objective is to show that speech variation discounted as "free" in previous linguistic descriptions is in fact systematic when social and situational factors are taken into account. On the basis of such information linguists have also traced previous linguistic change, and revealed trends predictively. Examples of this work include Labov (1972), Trudgill (1974, 1978), Bynon (1977: Ch. 5), Wolfram (1969) and Sankoff & Vincent (1977). Secular linguistic studies typically examine variation within a single language rather than bilingual behaviour.

One theoretical problem is that Labov treats speech as varying along a single stylistic continuum, from more dialectal to more standard. However, the Giles Accommodation Theory (see Chapter 6) predicts movement towards the regional norms (as well as the social variety) of interlocutors — in other words lateral as well as vertical movement in the Trudgill triangle (perhaps both at once) see figure overleaf.

There is no reason why this should not be taken into account within secular linguistic studies.

Method

Labov (1970) gives a clear and well-argued account of methodology in secular linguistics. Essentially the method recommended for data collec-

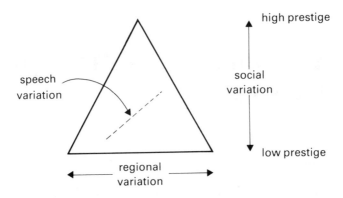

tion is the structured interview. The problem is to obtain recordings of sufficiently high quality to permit detailed phonetic analysis, along a stylistic range which includes the basilectal "vernacular". Labov (1970: 171) writes:

> "*Good data.* No matter what other methods may be used to obtain samples of speech (group sessions, anonymous observation), the only way to obtain sufficient good data on the speech of any one person is through an individual tape-recorded interview: that is through the most obvious kind of systematic observation. . . .
>
> There are some situations where candid recording is possible and permissable (*sic*), but the quality of the sound is so poor that such recordings are of confirmatory value at best."

A problem to which Labov devotes some discussion is the elicitation of samples of the speaker's vernacular — unguarded informal speech — in a formal interview situation. This Labov (1970) refers to as the "observer's paradox" — he writes:

> "We are then left with the OBSERVER'S PARADOX: the aim of linguistic research in the community must be to find out how people talk when they are not being systematically observed; yet we can only obtain this data by systematic observation."

Labov (1970) suggests a number of ingenious ways of circumventing this problem. Indeed, the interview has many advantages as a procedure for obtaining samples of more formal styles. However, recent technological innovations have to some extent mitigated the problems of obtaining high quality recordings in natural settings — see for example the use of radio microphones in Wells (1981: 6–7). In particular Milroy (1980) managed to obtain recordings of conversation in a natural environment of sufficient quality for very fine phonetic analysis. Furthermore, if the linguistic variable is not phonetic but grammatical or lexical recordings of this quality (and the structured interview) may not be necessary. However, Labov's insistence on hard data — recordings of real speech — remains a *sine qua non* of this type of research.

Model

The findings of secular linguistic studies are normally presented in probabilistic terms. In particular, use is made of "variable rules" — see Cedergren & Sankoff (1974). Such rules state that a linguistic variant occurs in a certain linguistic environment under certain conditions with a certain probability. Labov initially presented his findings as predictive, but later versions of the model overcame this shortcoming. Other forms of probabilistic statement used to describe linguistic patterning can be found in Milroy (1980). The use of statistical techniques such as Analysis of Variance enabled Milroy to show the significance of correlations between linguistic and social variation. In line with other behavioural sciences, it seems likely that sociolinguistics will make increasing use of statistical techniques and models.

Applying the Secular Linguistic Approach

The data base for this study is the collection of recordings of student conversation described in Chapter 3. When listening to this corpus I felt that some of the variation in admixture could possibly be interpreted if central sociolinguistic factors were taken into account, since certain types of speaker seemed to use more English and integrated items than others, and also certain topics seemed to exert influence on this process. This apparent link between linguistic variation and sociolinguistic factors demanded a secular linguistic approach. However, this study considerably extends the use of the approach since it examines natural bilingual conversation rather than elicited monolingual speech.

Variables Used in the Analysis

Component Elements of MIX

The dependent variables whose variation provided the main numerical base for the study were three component elements of MIX. These were Cantonese, integrated elements, and other contributions from English.

Cantonese was taken to include loanwords used by Cantonese monolinguals such as "ba sí" (bus) and "dik sí" (taxi). The *integrated elements* were the English elements heavily modified towards MIX norms which are described in Chapter 3: if there was any doubt whether items of English origin belonged to this category, a conservative approach was adopted and they were assigned to "English". *English* included both the relatively unassimilated academic specialist lexis and the comparatively rare elements of English intra-sentential rhetorical code-switching. On occasions these abbreviations are used: *c* – Cantonese; *i* – integrated items; *e* – other English elements.

Syllable Counting

An attempt is made in this study to explain variation in the proportions of *c*, *i* and *e* in terms of the contextual factors such as the sex of the speaker, topic, etc. The variation was quantified by counting syllables of the three component elements. So, for example, the utterance "ngóh lam *English* hóu sō fú" (I think English is a soft option) contains 3 syllables of Cantonese, two of English and two syllables of "integrated items". Such syllable counts were recorded in association with topics, speakers and groups. So, for example, one conversation was analysed as follows.

TABLE 9   *Topic 5*

		Topic 02			Topic 03			Topic 10		
		i	*e*	*c*	*i*	*e*	*c*	*i*	*e*	*c*
Speaker A	first speech on topic	4	3	82	12	12	118	2	11	91
	second speech on topic				25	12	204	13	7	175
	total # of syllables	4	3	82	37	24	322	15	18	266
Speaker B	first speech on topic	–	6	104	10	15	211	12	19	196
	second speech on topic				–	2	26	–	–	46
	total # of syllables	–	6	104	10	17	237	12	19	242

Syllable counting was adopted because it provides an easily quantifiable way of assessing the variation in the proportions of the three elements. Such counts do not have numerical significance, since English and Cantonese words probably do not have the same number of syllables. However, if one is examining *variation* in proportions from one context to another, then this is not a problem. Syllable counting in Cantonese is not difficult, since the language is clearly segmented into syllables, and in transcriptions one Chinese character consistently represents one syllable. Similarly the integrated elements are sufficiently close in phonological nature to Cantonese to cause little difficulty in counting. Students' pronunciation of English, under the influence of Cantonese, usually segments words clearly, but in case of doubt a conservative policy was adopted and the minimum number of syllables was recorded. This provided adequate consistency in the examination of variation in the proportion of syllables.

Independent Variables

A number of factors were tested to see whether they were associated with variation in the composition of MIX. These were the topic of the conversation, the influence of the group of speakers, and the individual characteristics of each speaker — sex, secondary schooling, and the type of academic subject s/he was studying. The group variable consists of the difference between the group of speakers found on one tape and each group found on other tapes, controlling for sex, schooling, topic and academic subject. The secondary schools were divided into four types on a scale from 1 (most prestigious) to 4 (least prestigious). Schools were allocated to these categories on the basis of an *ad hoc* questionnaire circulated to a number of Chinese colleagues and to lecturers in the School of Education at Hong Kong University. Schooling was thought to be important firstly because code mixing behaviour often has its origins in schools, and secondly because school type may correlate with social class and degree of westernization of the individual (see Gibbons, 1982 and 1984, for the importance of schooling in language behaviour and the variable prestige of Hong Kong secondary schools). The type of academic subject had no measurable effect so it will not be discussed further. The categories for sex were (1) male and (2) female. Topic was divided into eight categories which had proved useful in previous studies. These were: (1) academic content (i.e. discussing academic Philosophy, Statistics etc.) (2) current affairs, world view, religion (3) student social and political life (4) secondary school (5) leisure outside the university and home (6) formulaic utterances, contentless speech, uncategorizable speech (7) basics (food, clothing, health, sex, transport, etc.) (8) general academic (university administration, timetables, etc.)

Statistical Model

The coded data were processed with the help of Bacon-Shone.[1] His description of the linear statistical procedure, and the findings in statistical form are available in Appendix 4. The findings are adjusted — for example, when assessing groups we controlled for the effects of topic, sex and school.

Results

The linear model showed that more than half of the variation in the composition of MIX may be explained by four factors: group, topic, school and sex. Other factors were not useful. Group and topic are considerably stronger, with school and sex able to account for much less variation. These findings are available in statistical form in Appendix 4. They can be displayed and discussed more easily in the form of plots, in which the (fitted) proportions of syllables are plotted for each value of the independent variables. Since we are treating three linguistic components in MIX, three axes are required (the length of the three axes naturally always add up to the same figure). The form of the plots is therefore triangular; the axes of the plots are the following:

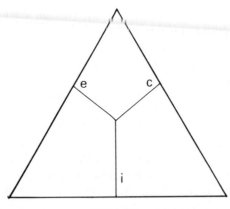

FIGURE 7

An increase in a particular component of MIX is displayed by a lengthened axis for that component. So, for example, in Figure 8 variable A is associated with a higher proportion of English and less integrated items or Cantonese compared to variable B which is associated with more integrated items and Cantonese, and with a reduced amount of English.

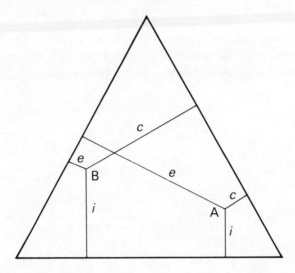

FIGURE 8

The triangles are all taken from the bottom, left-hand ⅑ of a larger triangle. Owing to the numerical dominance of Cantonese lexis in the conversations, all variation takes place there: the triangles consist of the shaded segment in this diagram:

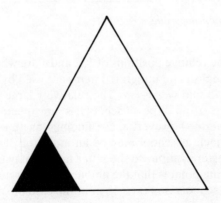

FIGURE 9

Let us then look at the four factors which appear to have some bearing on the composition of MIX, looking first at the two relatively unimportant ones.

School

The prestige of the speaker's secondary school is the basis of the categorization (see 'Independent Variables' pp. 95). The categories run from 1 – most prestigious schools, to 4 – least prestigious schools.

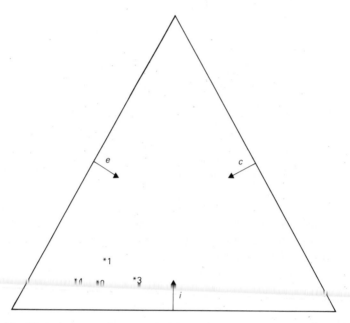

FIGURE 10   *Variation according to school*

In the diagram the relative positions of 1, 2 and 4 are what might have been predicted: less English and integrated items are used by speakers from less prestigious schools and *vice versa*. The relatively large amount of English used by speakers from type 3 schools is unexpected and difficult to interpret. In general, however, these findings on the role of school are interesting inasmuch as school may be an indicator of social class origins and degree of westernization, so the latter factors may underlie this effect. Another interesting point is that the amount of integrated lexis used by the most prestigious schools is greater than in the case of speakers from other schools: this may be an indication that the integration process is being led by the most prestigious and westernized group. However, if this plot is compared with those for topic and group it is apparent that school makes considerably less difference to the proportions of contributions from the donor codes.

Sex

The variables are 1 – male, and 2 – female, and refer to the sex of the speaker.

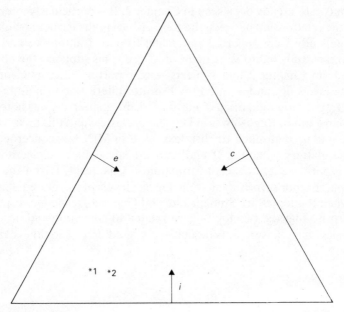

FIGURE 11   *Variation according to the sex of the speaker*

Since the gap between the two variables is small, not too much significance should be attached to the finding. What difference there is would appear to indicate that the sexes use almost the same amount of *i*, but females use more English and less Cantonese. This is interesting given the prestige and "fashionable" and "modern" implications of the use of English (see Chapter 6). The findings may reflect those of Trudgill (1972), Smith (1979) and others who have found a tendency among female speakers towards greater use of prestige linguistic forms. Ellen Ryan (1979: 155) writes, "it appears that male-female differences in attitudes exist with males tending to respond more to peer group pressures ... and females inclined to respond more to the advantages for social advancement".

Topic

The topics were the following (see also Independent Variables p. 95): 1 – academic content; 2 – current affairs, world view, religion; 3 – student life; 4 – secondary school; 5 – leisure outside university and home; 6 – formulaic utterances, contentless speech, other; 7 – basics; 8 – general academic.

The salience of topic as an influence on the behaviour of this speech community has already been seen in Chapter 2. It is particularly interesting to note the relationship between the topics which in the earlier Sociology of Language study were reported as leading to pure Cantonese, and those which in this study led to *increased* Cantonese. This supports the observation made in Chapter 2 that subjects were reporting MIX as Cantonese when the levels of i and e were low. It is also interesting to note the high level of English found in discussions of academic matters: it was noted that the principal use of English was in University classes, and this links up both with the finding that much English lexis used in MIX was concerned with academic matters (Chapter 3) and with the speculations concerning the role of experience and concept formation in Chapter 4. Given the latter discussion, it is not surprising that the highest levels of integrated items are found when the topics are Student Life and General Academic. Equally it is no surprise that the two topics least related to education and university life, "basics" and "leisure outside university and home" should evoke very

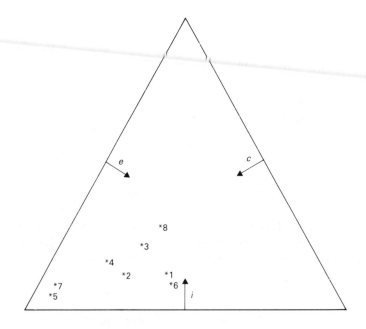

FIGURE 12   *Variation according to topic*

little *i* and *e*. Finally, since students have been educated partly in English, serious matters such as current affairs and religion involve some use of English, but few integrated items.

The findings on the effect of topic reflect well the three milieux (or domains) discussed in the word association experiment. It appears that integrated lexis is indeed associated with the domain of student life: other English is associated with the academic domain: and Cantonese with the Chinese life led outside the University context.

Group

The data base for this study consisted of a number of tape recordings, each made by a different group of speakers. As Figure 12 shows there were considerable differences in the overall composition of the speech of these different groups even allowing for the effects of topic, sex and schooling. The strength of the group effect is interesting, and is open to a number of interpretations. One is that there are influences upon the behaviour of the group which have not been included in the model, in particular the role of group dynamics (see below). It is likely that this explains some of the

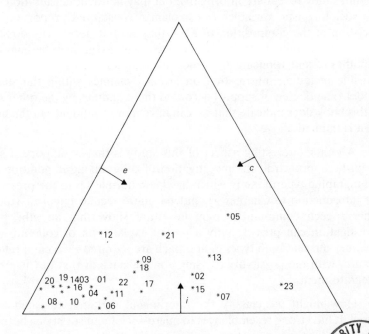

FIGURE 13 *Variation according to group*

variation and this acts as a reminder that excessive claims should not be made for studies such as this. In addition, however, a possible interpretation of the group effect can be drawn from the recent work of Giles and others in the social psychology of language. According to the Giles accommodation theory (Giles & Powesland, 1975: 155–80) there is a strong tendency for people to modify their speech towards that of their interlocutors to establish solidarity. In a group this could lead to the members reaching some form of consensus on the nature of the group's speech (a "linguistic wavelength"), with more powerful or forceful group members possibly exerting more influence. In the case of MIX the linguistic wavelength (which still permits individual variation) involves the levels of contribution from each component code. Various papers in Heller (forthcoming) discuss the role of group dynamics in code choice, and see also Scotton's (1983) maxims.

Evaluating a Secular Linguistic Approach to Code-Mixing

There is a fundamental problem in many probabilistic studies in that the links they reveal are informative but may not denote causation. While the sociolinguistic variables *can* explain a substantial proportion of the variation in the composition of MIX they do not necessarily do so. The solution (not applied in this study) is once again to set these findings up as a hypothesis, and replicate the study on another set of conversations, if possible including information on group dynamics within the statistical model. The degree of support accorded these findings by the other studies in this book does indicate that we can have more confidence in the findings than is implied above.

Another interesting aspect of this study is that it supports a secular linguistic approach to the investigation of code-mixing in addition to the ethnographic type of study which has been normal up to the present (see the introduction to Chapter 4). Indeed, more secular linguistic studies in other speech communities may in future show that an ethnographic investigation can provide only a partial explanation of code-mixing behaviour, and that both types of approach are required for a comprehensive picture, with the possibility of using a model such as that in Chapter 7 to integrate them.

How might we classify the interlingual variation revealed by this study? It has strong resemblances to micro-sociolinguistic style-shifting and Labovian language variation on the one hand. However, this approach usually examines variation with a single language, it is intralingual rather than interlingual. This type of language behaviour is also related to code-switching approaches which handle the use of more than one language, but traditionally deal with shifts from one language to another rather than a change of degree or amounts of the contributions of several codes to a code mixture. The variation in the composition of MIX might therefore be termed "code-swaying", defined as *variation in the composition of code mixtures according to one or more sociolinguistic factors*. Since code-swaying falls between traditional macro- and micro-sociolinguistic categories, it adds weight to Bell's (1976) call for an integration of macro- and micro-sociolinguistics in a general theory of sociolinguistics, perhaps even of language behaviour.

In Chapter 3 I suggested the MIX may be an incipient language mixed koiné (following Hymes, 1971a: 78–79). If this is so then this code-swaying study may give an idea of the role of central sociolinguistic factors in the processes of language change which have been important in shaping languages such as English, Japanese and Modern Hebrew.

Note to Chapter 5

1. I should like to thank Dr John Bacon-Shone of the Statistics Department, University of Hong Kong for his invaluable help.

6 A Social-Psychological Matched Guise Approach

Introduction

This approach is associated most strongly with Lambert and Giles. It had its origins in the work of Lambert, Tucker and others on Canadian bilingualism (e.g. Lambert, Frankel & Tucker, 1966; Lambert *et al.*, 1960; Gardner & Taylor, 1968). This work has continued, and been complemented by work done in many other societies — see, for instance, Giles & St. Clair (1979). The principal contribution of the social psychology of language to our understanding of code-switching concerns the meaning of code choices. Researchers have looked at the social and interpersonal effects produced by the choice of particular languages, dialects and accents within speech communities. For example, when a French Canadian switches to English, this may give an impression of competence and prestige, while a switch to French may be seen as an assertion of French ethnicity and values. A useful theory that has emerged from this work is the Giles Accommodation Theory (see Giles & Powesland, 1975: Ch. 9). To simplify somewhat, this theory states that speakers modify their speech towards that of interlocutors to decrease social distance, and *vice versa*.

Method

Most studies in the social psychology of language are experimental, the most common type being the *matched guise experiment*. In this experiment subjects are asked to rate speakers on a number of traits, using Lickert judgement scales of this type.

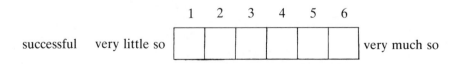

104

The voices heard by the subjects speak more than one code. Subjects are not informed that they in fact hear the same speaker more than once, using each code (the speakers are bilingual/bivarietal). This controls for nearly all factors, leaving code as the only major variable. One can thus elicit from subjects the effects caused by the use of the codes in question.

Model

The results of matched guise studies are analysed and presented in statistical form. Statistical correlations between codes and traits are displayed, thus enabling the researcher to characterize the codes using specific traits. A further common step is to use the sophisticated statistical technique of factor analysis with rotation. This opens the possibility of finding "factors" into which the traits group: for example, scores on scales such as "rich", "good-looking" and "successful" might be shown to co-vary, and to comprise a single factor that could be termed "prestige". Such statistical techniques can also be used in other types of sociolinguistic studies (e.g. Milroy, 1980).

Applying the Matched Guise Approach

Language attitudes in Hong Kong were discussed in Chapter 1. To summarize briefly, both matched guise studies (including Lyczak, Fu & Ho, 1976) and surveys (e.g. Pierson, Fu & Lee, 1980, and Cheng et al., 1973) have shown positive affective attitudes towards Chinese, and some discomfort with regard to English, although prestige is attached to a knowledge of the latter. MIX has received scant attention in attitude studies in Hong Kong.

MIX has been shown to be common in student-student interaction, while the use of spoken English among Chinese is stigmatized. In Chapters 3 and 4 a case was made for regarding MIX as an alternative code choice alongside English and Cantonese (c.f. Elías-Olivares, 1979). It was demonstrated that MIX is not used only when necessary in communicating ideas, as this can often be done adequately in pure Cantonese: this parallels Rayfield's (1970) findings with regard to the mixing of English and Yiddish. The only evidence concerning attitudes toward MIX is found in the responses to a few items in a questionnaire administered by Kwok, Chan & Sun (1972: 70–72). Among their student sample 80.5% admitted to using MIX, while at the same time 39.5% found the use of MIX irritating. This apparent dislike of MIX is echoed in anecdotal statements by other bilinguals, and insult terms used to describe this form of language behaviour. It appears, therefore, that there may be a conflict between expressed antipathy to MIX, and actual behaviour, in which MIX is common (more so than necessary for communication of ideas). Since there were no empirical studies of attitudes to MIX, a matched guise study was undertaken to examine this paradox. It investigated the attitudes of student bilinguals towards the use of MIX by their fellows.

The hypothesis was that while bilinguals had an *overt* attitude of hostility towards MIX, they also held positive *covert* attitudes towards it. ("Covert" attitudes to language behaviour are discussed by Trudgill, 1972, who found that contrary to expectations some middle class males in Norwich were well disposed towards working class speech norms. He concluded that working class speech had "covert" or hidden prestige for this group. See also Edwards, 1979.) Three alternative hypotheses were advanced concerning the nature of covert attitudes towards MIX. Firstly, since MIX has certain features unique to the student speech community, MIX might be a marker of student identity and solidarity. Friendly & Glucksberg (1970: 55) found such a phenomenon in the speech of students at Princeton University: they write: "the students have developed an extensive idiosyncratic lexicon which is not familiar to outsiders" (the parallels with MIX are evident) and continue "one indicant of an individual's acquisition of membership in a sub-culture is his acquisition of the connotative and denotative meanings of the words that are unique to the sub-culture's specific lexicon." The second hypothesis was that MIX denotes status. While there is considerable evidence that English is prestigious, there appears to be a social norm opposing its spoken use among Chinese (see above). MIX is predominantly Cantonese, which should neutralize this norm, while the admixture of English may enable the speaker to attract the prestige connotations of the latter. The marking of membership of the university speech community may also be a status factor, in that students are often seen as an élite group in Hong Kong. A third possibility was that the use of MIX is a "strategy of neutrality" (as discussed in Scotton, 1976), enabling speakers to avoid appearing either totally Chinese or totally Western in orientation.

The study also attempted to discover whether the matched guise technique can be used to probe covert attitudes which conflict with expressed views, in a situation such as Hong Kong's where language is an emotional and political issue.

Method[1]

Previous matched-guise studies of covert attitudes have had limited success (Ryan, 1979). Ryan suggests that part of the problem may derive from the methods used, inasmuch as insufficient attention may have been paid to the social context of speech—i.e. the appropriacy of a certain code or style to certain situations. MIX is used predominantly in relaxed conversational settings. To ensure that subjects were aware that MIX was an appropriate choice of code in the recorded material, several steps were taken. The first was to extract the content of all the speech used (by the guise voices) from a recording of a genuine MIX conversation. This conversation was then divided into three segments (see rationale below), and Cantonese and English versions were produced. (The conversation was also slightly modified so that the speaker whose voice was to be assessed did most of the talking.) The second step was to tell subjects that they were listening to recordings of genuine conversations: for this fiction to be maintained each segment could be heard only once; the normal matched-guise procedure of reading aloud the same passage in different languages would have destroyed any claim to authenticity, and would have placed the recordings in the formal domain where MIX is less appropriate.

A consequence of the above was that it was necessary to control for the effects of the three segments upon judgements. For reasons to be discussed below, other factors which had to be taken into account were the language in which the instructions were given (3 possibilities—English, MIX, Cantonese), and the sex of the speaker (2). With the three guise languages and three segments this gave a $3 \times 3 \times 3 \times 2$ factorial design for the investigation. To establish discrete cells in which each variable occurred once with each other would have required many cells, entailing unmanageable complexity and an unrealistically large homogeneous sample. Instead, a modified randomized block design was used, in which mutual influences were confounded by randomizing other treatments within each variable. Hence the main effect of each variable could be looked at in isolation, since all other variables had been rotated against it. This design had the disadvantage that interactions could not be studied as there was confounding.

Stimulus Material

The subjects listened to one of three tape recordings, and scored the guise voices on twenty rating scales (see *Measures* below). The three tapes were as follows:

Language of Instructions	Main Speaker	Segment	Guise Language
	(A (male)	II	Cantonese
	(		
Tape 1 English	(B (female)	I	MIX
	(		
	(A	III	English
	(B	III	MIX
	(		
Tape 2 MIX	(A	I	Cantonese
	(		
	(B	II	English
	(		
	(B	I	English
	(		
Tape 3 Cantonese	(A	II	MIX
	(		
	(B	III	Cantonese

One can observe that each level of each variable occurs in conjunction with each level of all other variables. The variables were as follows:

Language of Instructions

As noted previously, Yang & Bond (1980), Bond & Yang (1982) and Pierson & Bond (1982) working in Hong Kong have found that the language in which experiments are conducted can have a significant effect upon subjects' reactions. To examine (and control) for such effects, the instructions and introduction were all given on the tapes by one speaker, using a different language on each tape. Consequently, three tapes and three matched groups were used. Other steps taken: when the Language of the Instructions was English, the rating scales were in English only. When the Language of the Instructions was MIX or Cantonese, the rating scales were bilingual in English and written Chinese (monolingual Chinese scales were avoided as translation equivalents are rarely exact). The people running the experiment were a Westerner and a Chinese. Both said as little as possible, since the instructions were on the tape.

Guise Voices

There were two main Guise Voices; both belonged to university students, one male and one female. Both sexes were included as there is a well-attested tendency for females to use more prestige markers in speech

(Smith, 1979). Early statistical processing of the data revealed that there was no significant difference in assessment of the two voices, and that the sex of the listeners was also not significant. The order of speakers was varied to reduce influence from that source.

Segments

As described above, a piece of genuine MIX conversation was divided into three segments of approximately 30 seconds in length, and trilingual versions were prepared. The recordings of these were judged to be "naturalistic" by 19 native speakers in a pilot experiment.

Guise Languages

The subjects were asked to judge speakers using three languages: English, MIX and Cantonese. Since the recordings were supposedly of natural conversations among students, they were made by university students, and the English was accented. Subjects were asked to ignore the language and judge the personality solely by voice: however, hearing only three voices, each using a different code, may have brought language to the attention of subjects, possibly tapping conscious attitudes to the codes in question.

Measures

To avoid excessive pre-judgement, Likert scales were used which attempted to examine not only solidarity and status, but also Chineseness, Westernization and education (for some of the tortured relationships between language and education in Hong Kong, see Gibbons, 1982). These scales derived from (a) previous matched-guise studies (especially Giles & Powesland, 1975; Ryan & Carranza, 1975; Lyczak, Fu & Ho, 1976); (b) a simple questionnaire given to 24 post-graduate students asking for the characteristics of "a typical Chinese", "a good friend", "a well educated person", and (c) intuitions of the author derived from earlier research. Originally 30 scales with seven points were constructed; ten scales which were considered evaluatively inconsequential in a pilot study were eliminated. The scales used were the following: helpful; well-mannered and polite; friendly; successful; kind; knowledgeable; good-looking; understanding; ambitious; proud—humble; confident—timid; modern—traditional; gentle—aggressive; authoritarian—timid; idealistic —realistic; a show-off—modest; narrow-minded—broad-minded; clothes: fashionable—unfashionable; school: unknown—famous; cultural orientation: Chinese—Western. The relationship of the scales to the major traits was as follows:

status: successful, good-looking, ambitious, confident, school (famous), clothes (fashionable) (N.B. some of these may also reflect Westernization);
solidarity: helpful, friendly, understanding, gentle, kind;
Chineseness: humble, traditional, realistic, modest, cultural orientation (Chinese);
educated: broad-minded, liberal, knowledgeable, well mannered and polite, idealistic, school (famous);

The adjectives in "educated" and "Chineseness" were mostly derived from the questionnaire. These factors did not all emerge from the results.

Listener Characteristics

The subjects were undergraduates at the University of Hong Kong, studying in the Faculties of Social Science (66 subjects) and Arts (33 subjects), and this 2:1 ratio was maintained when they were divided into matched-groupings to listen to the tapes. There were 52 female and 46 male subjects, with one person's sex not being recorded. At the end of the experiment, they were asked to rate themselves on two seven-point scales: During the experiment how did you feel? (very uncomfortable...very comfortable); What is your cultural orientation? (Chinese—Western). The first was intended to monitor the subjects' reaction to the experiment, the second their level of Westernization. These listener characteristics proved to be of little or no significance in early statistical processing of the data and will not be discussed further.

Procedure

With the permission of lecturers, tapes were played in classes using the first 10 minutes of a tutorial or lecture hour. Rating sheets were distributed and the recording played. All instructions were given on the tape, and the experimenters (one Western, one Chinese) said very little, Subjects were asked to tick one of seven boxes on the 20 rating scales, repeating the procedure for each guise voice; they then noted down the personal information mentioned in Listener Characteristics previously.

Results

The main effects on the adjective scores of the three Guise Languages and the three Languages of the Instructions were computed using Analysis of Variance. The effect of the Guise Languages was significant on 14 scales. In addition, *t* tests were used to examine differences between pairs of languages in order to determine which language was significantly different from which on these fourteen scales. (The confidence intervals for the differences between mean scores were also tested at the 95% level, following Edwards, 1977: 85–86: the null hypothesis could be rejected for all significant cases.) On the basis of these tests, the scales are divided into four groups—Figures 14–17. The charts of the main effects of the guise languages which follow display the F ratios, significances and plots of the means (which reveal the direction of movement).

In Figure 14, we can see that a person who uses MIX rather than English or Cantonese is seen as more ill-mannered and more prone to "showing off"—essentially negative evaluations.

In Figure 15, we can observe that students speaking either MIX or Cantonese are viewed as lacking in knowledge, good looks and idealism, compared to those speaking English.

From the results presented in Figure 16, it can be seen that MIX receives the following judgements in common with English and in contrast to Cantonese: more ambitious, proud, confident, prestigious school, and modern.

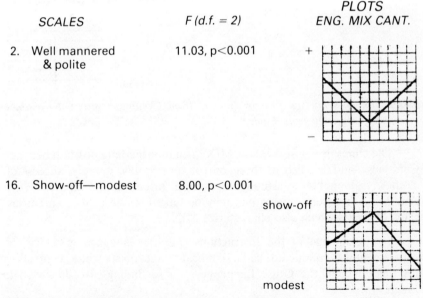

		PLOTS
SCALES	*F (d.f. = 2)*	*ENG. MIX CANT.*
2. Well mannered & polite	11.03, p<0.001	+
16. Show-off—modest	8.00, p<0.001	show-off ... modest

FIGURE 14   *Mix significantly different from English and Cantonese: English not significantly different from Cantonese*

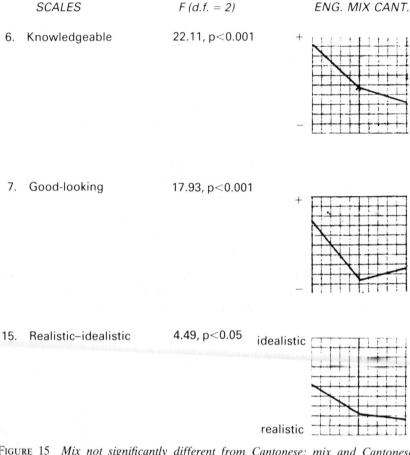

SCALES	F (d.f. = 2)	ENG. MIX CANT.
6. Knowledgeable	22.11, p<0.001	+
7. Good-looking	17.93, p<0.001	+
15. Realistic–idealistic	4.49, p<0.05	idealistic ... realistic

FIGURE 15 *Mix not significantly different from Cantonese: mix and Cantonese significantly different from English*

The clines in Figure 17 show MIX in an intermediate position between Cantonese and English in three out of four scales, namely, successful, clothes: fashionable-unfashionable, cultural orientation: Chinese—Western. The other item, aggressive, may be linked to the proud, ambitious, show off traits which also characterize MIX.

The Language of the Instructions (i.e. the language in which the experiment was conducted) had a significant effect on six scales, controlling for the effect of the Guise Languages. These findings are displayed in Figure 18.

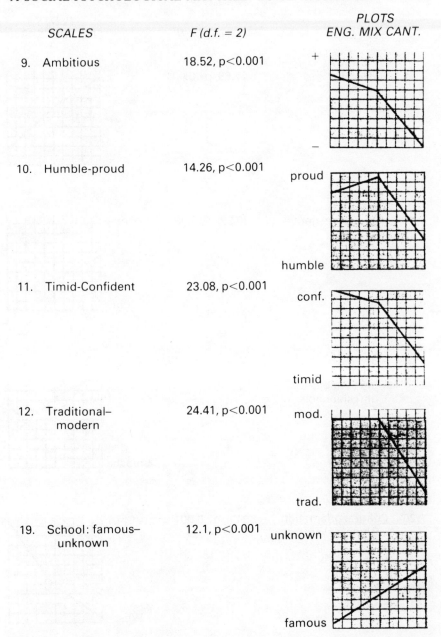

FIGURE 16   *Mix not significantly different from English: mix and English significantly different from Cantonese*

SCALES	F (d.f. = 2)	PLOTS ENG. MIX CANT.

4. Successful   27.69, p<0.001   +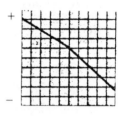

13. Aggressive–gentle   30.92, p<0.001   gentle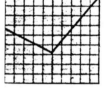

                                                    aggr.

18. Clothes: 17.19, p<0.001   fash.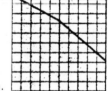
    fashionable–
    unfashionable

                                                    unfash.

20. Cultural orientation: 34.4, p<0.001   Chi.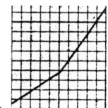
    Chinese–Western

                                                    West.

FIGURE 17   Continua: all three Guise Languages significantly different

Comparing the plots for the language of the Instructions (Figure 18) with those for the Guise Languages (Figures 14–17), it can be seen that the relative positions of English and Cantonese are little changed. The relative position of MIX is considerably different, however, with more favourable judgements on most scales. The consistency of this finding is interesting, but its interpretation is problematic, involving as it does the impact of the Language of the Instructions upon judgements of the Guise Languages.

The scores on the rating scales were also subjected to a Principal Components Analysis with Varimax rotation; that is, their internal co-variation was analysed to isolate any underlying factors. Four major factors were found which could account for over half of the variation. The first, which could account for 24.9% of the total variation, consisted of the following: unhelpful, ill-mannered, unfriendly, unkind, lacking in under-standing and narrow minded. This appears to be a "reversed" solidarity measure, showing dislike. It has therefore been assigned the name "antipathy". The second factor, which could account for 19.3% of the total variation, showed the following components most strongly: humble, timid, gentle and modest. This factor appears to be a "humility" factor, and as humility is a distinguishing Chinese characteristic it might be termed "Chinese humility". The third factor, which could explain 6.2% of the variation, contained the negative end of these scales: successful, know-ledgeable, good-looking, ambitious. This appears therefore to be a "re-versed" status factor. A fourth factor, which could explain 5.4% of the variation, appeared to be a reversed "Westernization" factor, consisting of the negative end of: modern, cultural orientation—Western, school—famous, clothes—fashionable. (One should perhaps mention here that in Hong Kong "modern" is a euphemism for "Western", that fashionable clothes are by definition Western, and that most famous schools tend to westernize their students.)

The factor scores derived from this Principal Components Analysis were then subjected to a univariate Analysis of Variance, the independ-ence variables being the Guise Languages and the Languages of the Instruction (each having 3 levels—English, MIX and Cantonese). The results are given in Figure 19.

Because the first factor "antipathy" was heavily contaminated by others, using the factor scores did not provide significant results. This factor was therefore computed using an unweighted cumulation of the relevant scales only (see Figure 19, Part B): this produced clear and significant results.

PLOTS
ENG. MIX CANT.

F (d.f. = 2)

SCALES

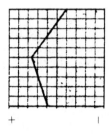

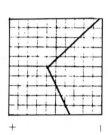

4. Successful — $.73, p<0.001$

6. Knowledgeable — $7.6, p<0.001$

7. Good-looking — $2.94, p<0.001$

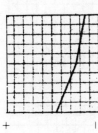
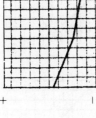

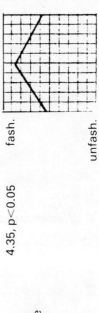
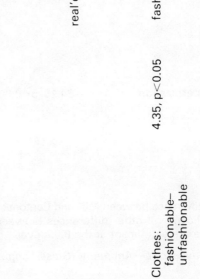
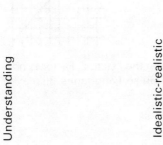

8. Understanding 3.29, p<0.05

15. Idealistic-realistic 5.53, p<0.01

18. Clothes:
fashionable–
unfashionable 4.35, p<0.05

FIGURE 18 *Main effects – Languages of the Instructions*

FACTORS	F (d.f. = 2)	PLOTS ENG. MIX CANT.
1. Antipathy	n.s.	
2. Chinese humility	16.04, p<0.001	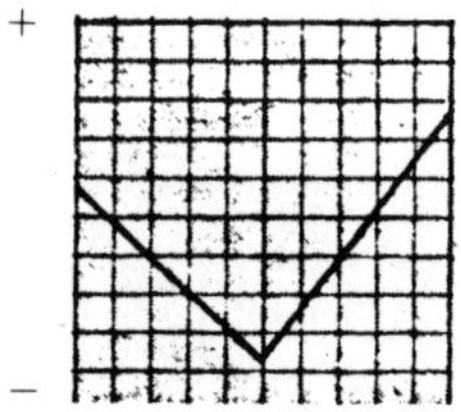
3. Status	24.65, p<0.001	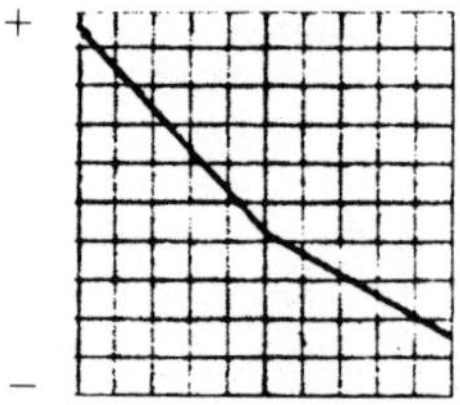
4. Westernization	24.15, p<0.001	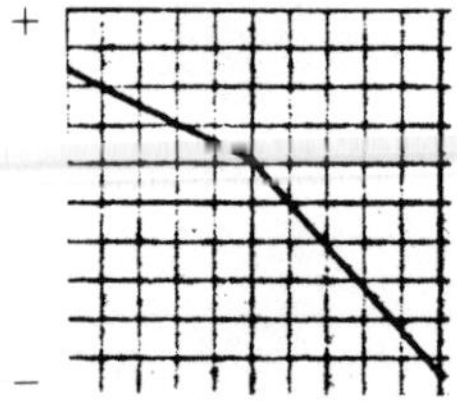

N.B. The difference between MIX and Cantonese on the "status" Factor is not significant: all other differences between Guise Languages displayed above are significant at the 0.05 level.

B. *Cumulative Scale—Antipathy (Guise Languages)*

13.08, p<0.001

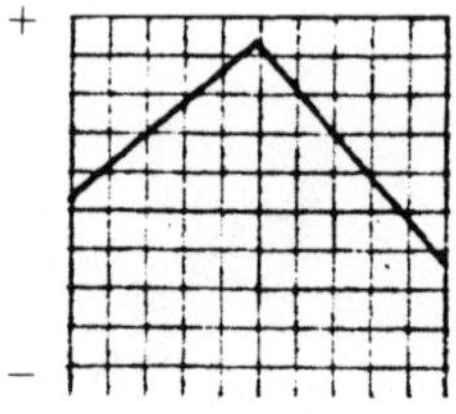

FIGURE 19 A. *Main effects of factors for Guise Languages*

In the results for main effects of the Guise Languages, one can observe that Cantonese is associated with "Chinese humility" and low "Westernization", and English with "status" and "Westernization". MIX is most strongly characterized by "antipathy", and by a lack of "Chinese humility"—arrogance? It does, however, score more highly than Cantonese on the status and Westernization factors which may provide a clue to possible covert attitudes.

The main effects of the Language of the Instructions are of some interest. (See Figure 20). On factor 3 MIX is associated most strongly with status, while the finding for factor 4 is that MIX is highest on the factor of Westernization.

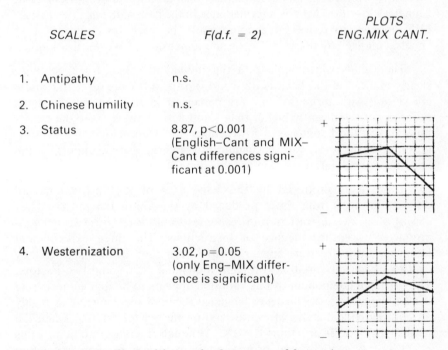

SCALES	F(d.f. = 2)	PLOTS ENG.MIX CANT.
1. Antipathy	n.s.	
2. Chinese humility	n.s.	
3. Status	8.87, p<0.001 (English–Cant and MIX–Cant differences significant at 0.001)	
4. Westernization	3.02, p=0.05 (only Eng–MIX difference is significant)	

FIGURE 20   *Main effects of factors for Languages of Instruction*

Discussion

These findings confirm those of Lyczak, Fu & Ho (1976) with regard to attitudes towards Cantonese and English. They indicate that, when Chinese speakers use English to one another, they give an impression of status and Westernization. When they use Cantonese, they give an impression of Chinese humility and solidarity.

This study's main focus was attitudes towards MIX; in particular, the conflict between expressed attitudes of hostility towards MIX, and its frequent use. The ratings of the Guise Languages on the individual scales (Figures 14–17) show that MIX's unique attributes are negative, and that it attracts only negative attributes of Cantonese. The overt hostility mentioned in the introduction is displayed in a number of negative judgements: ill-mannered, a "show-off", ignorant, not good-looking, aggressive and proud (this might be summarized as ugly-ignorant-arrogance). However, when we turn to attributes shared with English, they are not, with the possible exception of "proud", essentially negative. Rather, they appear to accord confidence and status to the user of MIX. On the three traits, successful, clothes: fashionable—unfashionable, and cultural orientation: Chinese—Western, MIX is intermediate. In the case of the last two ratings MIX appears to represent a compromise between East and West—a "neutral choice" (Scotton, 1976) on the dimension of Westernization.

The trends which appear in the individual scales are even more clearly marked in the Factors derived from them (Figure 19). MIX users are viewed with antipathy, and are perceived as arrogant. MIX's status rating is not significantly higher than Cantonese (however, see the results for status in the Language of Instructions discussed below). On Westernization, MIX is viewed as significantly intermediate, supporting the "neutral choice" interpretation for this dimension.

The effects produced by the Languages of the Instructions are different in type from those produced by the Guise Languages. They consist of an overall variation in responses to *all three* Guise Languages, produced by each Language of Instructions. The three experimental Languages of Instructions appear to tap differing sets of values, since they lead to significant variations on eight individual scales, and two Factors. The principal component of this variation appears to be that subjects rate the (student) voices (whichever language they are speaking) more highly on both individual status attributes and on the Factor "status" when the Language of the Instructions is MIX. Although the interpretation of this effect is problematic, it may provide additional evidence of an association between MIX and status.

Turning to the introductory hypothesis, it appears that MIX is indeed viewed with hostility, and a reason for this may be that mix speakers are perceived to be arrogant (Factor 2). Why, then, is MIX frequently used? The first hypothesis, that MIX is a marker of student solidarity, receives no support from this experiment. The second hypothesis, that MIX covertly attracts the status of English while avoiding social rules against using the latter, receives some support. On several individual status-related scales, English and MIX are not rated significantly different-ly. But on the Factor "status", MIX is rated on a par with Cantonese, lower than English. This may be mitigated by the Languages of the Instructions measure, wherein MIX induces a significantly higher status rating for all voices, possibly indicating that MIX is indeed statusful, but that this status is highly covert.

Turning to the third hypothesis, MIX is significantly intermediate both on individual Westernization scales and on the Factor "Westernization". The effects of the Languages of the Instructions on this Factor are marginally significant, which may show that the attribute "Westernization" is less covert than "status". These findings support the third hypothesis—that the use of MIX is a strategy of neutrality; speakers do not wish to appear totally westernized or uncompromisingly Chinese in orientation. This compromise probably reflects the degree of Westernization of most students, and could therefore be viewed as marking this element of their identity.

An interesting sidelight (suggested by Michael Bond) is thrown on these results by the work of Osgood and others (Osgood, Suci & Tannenbaum, 1957; Osgood, May & Miron, 1975) with the "semantic differential"—a concept developed from the study of word meanings. They use three main factors to describe semantic space—evaluation, potency, and activity (E.P.A.). The Principal Components Analysis revealed four factors; of these "antipathy" closely resembles "evaluation", "Chinese humility" resembles "activity", since humility and introversion occur within this factor for some Far Eastern samples; and "status" closely resembles "potency". The explanation of this correspondence is problema-tic. Is it possible that the use of different languages can in some undefined fashion "tap" different semantic elements? Is it possible that speakers are operating such a system when they code switch? Or is it simply the instrument and processing that produced this result? This area might repay further examination by psycho-linguists.

To summarize finally, while this study provides strong empirical support for the initial assumption that there is an attitude of hostility towards MIX in the student speech community, there is also firm evidence that the use of MIX marks a level of personal acculturation intermediate between Western and Chinese. Furthermore, there is some less firm empirical support for the hypothesis that MIX has covert status in this speech community. Hopefully, these approaches and findings will also throw light on attitudes in the many other communities in which mixed languages are both disliked and widely used.

Evaluating the Approach

The matched guise experiment has many advantages. It is a clever and subtle instrument capable of considerable variation, and it produces comparable numerical data. However, the experimental situation has potential problems similar to those of the structured interview. If one wishes to obtain relatively unconscious reactions to situated informal speech, the experimental setting may make this problematic. Nevertheless, researchers in this area have shown considerable ingenuity in overcoming such difficulties (see Giles & Bourhis, 1976). Another possible problem is that subjects may not be making judgements based on linguistic stimuli only; rather the linguistic stimuli may be cueing stereotypes. So while we may reveal attitudes to the use of the guise languages, these need not be simply and causally linked to the actual choice of the language in a conversation. However, the many studies of this type performed elsewhere support the view that some form of linkage does exist.

This particular matched guise experiment was quite successful in that attitudes to English and Cantonese were clearly revealed, as was hostility to MIX. However, the more covert attitudes to MIX were not revealed in a totally unequivocal way. This may point to a flaw in this particular experiment. Subjects heard only three extracts, each in a different code, which may have attracted conscious attention to the codes and thus revealed conscious rather than covert attitudes. Of some interest, however, was the contribution of the Language of the Instructions to the findings. This type of highly indirect and undetectable measure may have wider applications, although other studies are required before one could say with confidence that these are meaningful effects.

Note to Chapter 6

1. My thanks to Howard Giles for help in designing the experiment. Its idiosyncrasies are my own.

7 Speculative Conclusions

Introduction

In this chapter an attempt is made to step back from empirical data and to integrate the findings of the various studies in speculative theoretical and general conclusions. The study had three major objectives: 1) to evaluate in use a number of approaches from sociolinguistics and the social psychology of language; 2) to obtain information about the speech behaviour of students at the University of Hong Kong; and 3) to work towards a coherent model of code choice. Speculative conclusions concerning each of these are presented in turn in the three sections which follow.

Reflections on Models and Methods

The specific models and methods used in this study have been assessed individually in their respective chapters. However, since scholars sometimes view different approaches as in some sense conflicting, it is worth indicating that here the varied approaches have not clashed. Rather they have proved complementary, each producing additional information, and at the same time providing a measure of mutual support and confirmation. If the researcher can master a very natural tendency to understate weaknesses in findings this can provide a valuable filter through which to view research results. The advantage of a multidimensional study of the language behaviour of a single group is that the strengths of one approach may help to compensate for the weaknesses in another. Thus researchers may find themselves in the fortunate position of being reasonably content with overall findings, while having distinct reservations concerning component studies.

Speculations on Student Bilingualism at the University of Hong Kong

Societal Bilingualism

Hong Kong, by virtue of its status as a British colony on the Chinese coast, forms a confluence of two great cultural traditions. It is therefore predictable that the local culture should show influences from both sources, although the Chinese element appears dominant. However, Hong Kong is not simply an amalgam of East and West. Hong Kong people and culture (particularly of the under 30 age group) are distinct and identifiable — a cursory introduction to Hong Kong cinema or pop music would make this apparent. The local society has developed unique characteristics in a similar fashion to some creole societies, although the latter rarely have a similarly dominant native cultural component. Nevertheless, it must be acknowledged that many Hong Kong people would reject the view that they are "culturally mixed" or that they are basically "Hong Kongers": they perceive themselves primarily as "Chinese".

Sociolinguistics has demonstrated in many societies the ways in which culture is mirrored in language. A cultural perspective may therefore help in providing a speculative interpretation of the speech behaviour of the students at three main levels discussed in this research. These are:

1. the very frequent choice of MIX, rather than English or Cantonese with fellow bilinguals;
2. the composition of MIX;
3. attitudes towards MIX.

Looking first at(2.), the composition of MIX, we see a code which is predominantly Chinese, with admixture from English: the parallel with the local culture as described above is apparent. Add to this the evidence both of a unique and partly rule-governed system for mixing and also of elements unique to MIX, and similarities to the local culture (predominantly Chinese, with Western admixture and some unique elements) become striking. Turning to (3.), attitudes, the matched guise study showed overt hostility to MIX, allied to a covert recognition of an identity neither Eastern nor Western. Again, this parallels the attitudes towards local culture and behaviour outlined in the preceding paragraph. This putative role of MIX, as the expression of a consciously rejected identity, may also go some way towards explaining the very frequent choice of MIX (1.), despite expressed dislike of it.

Another perspective can be drawn from the system of symbols used in ethnicity studies — see for instance Postiglione (1983). The use of symbols in describing the Hong Kong situation is given in Table 10.

TABLE 10

Symbol	A	B	C
Linguistic Manifestation	Spoken Cantonese and Written Chinese	English	linguistic features unique to Hong Kong
Possible Associated Culture	Chinese	Western	Hong Kong

If a lower case character is used, this indicates a minor element. Obviously only a gross characterization is achieved, but this may prove helpful as a summary. The situation described in this thesis might be expressed as follows:

$$Ac + Bc + c$$

Linguistically this represents: Ac = Hong Kong Cantonese and Hong Kong written Chinese; Bc = Hong Kong English; c = MIX's unique features (the structure of the mixing mechanism, and some idiosyncratic elements). This may reflect the parallel cultural pattern: Ac = Hong Kong Chinese culture; Bc = Hong Kong Western culture; c = Hong Kong "modern" culture.

Although it is dangerous to do so, one might speculate that if political forces permit, one potential future for Hong Kong is one in which "c" becomes "C" writ large. In other words, it is possible to visualize the emergence of a Hong Kong culture and language, in which A elements, B elements and additional c elements combine in a distinctive fashion.

Domains

The concept of domain is defined by Fishman (1971b: 587) as follows:

"a socio-cultural construct abstracted from topics of communication, relationships between communicators, and locales of communication, in accord with the institutions of a society and the spheres of activity of a speech community."

This concept is developed, refined and exemplified in Fishman *et al.* (1971a). It has been criticized for its imprecision. Yet it is interesting to observe how well the concept applies through this book. At the level of simple code-switching, the use of English was linked almost exclusively to university instruction, and MIX to peer group interaction. The statistical study in Chapter 2 followed through on this theme, and the choice between MIX and Cantonese was associated with age, topic and style. Cantonese was found to be more common with non-peers, to discuss non-university activities, while MIX was more common with age peers, to discuss university life, in casual style. The study in Chapter 5 of "code swaying" — variation in the composition of MIX — revealed similar parameters. When conversing with fellow students, more English was used when discussing academic matters, more MIX words when discussing student life, and more Cantonese when discussing other matters. In other words, not only does the choice of code vary *in* situations, but the composition of the mixed code varies when *referring to* them. This accords well with Fishman's description of the effect of domains. In addition the word association experiment reported in Chapter 3 provides evidence for these domains having some form of psychological reality. So the three domains of peer/student life, academic study, and non-university, non-peer "Chinese" life are manifested in macro-sociolinguistic code choice, in micro-sociolinguistic variation, and in semantico-psychological organization of the lexicon. The very fact that these domains cross the boundaries between these varied sociolinguistic and psycholinguistic approaches calls for a more integrated model of language behaviour. The concept of "domain" permits an economical yet convincing portrayal of a major element in student speech behaviour: it is of value as a descriptive tool. More tendentiously, one could say that the results of these studies provide empirical support for the reality of "domains" in language behaviour.

Individual Bilingualism

The individual bilingualism of students at the University of Hong Kong can be classified as "functional bilingualism". Baetens Beardsmore (1982: 9–10) makes the important point that it is hard to define, and even harder to find, true "ambilingualism" — i.e. a perfect mastery of two languages. The reality is that speakers will tend to cope better with some aspects of their life in one or other of their languages. In the case of the samples used in this study, we have seen that much of their non-academic, non-student life is mediated through Chinese. However, in Chapter 4, it was noted that English academic lexis is more available even though Chinese equivalents are often known, so English might be said to have some sort of dominance in the academic domain. English is subordinate, and less fluent than Cantonese in other areas. In addition there is a MIX competence, which involves a knowledge of MIX lexis and expressions, and control of the sytems used to integrate items at the phonological and syntactic levels.

The problem with the approach taken in most studies of individual bilingualism is that it assumes essentially that the codes within the speaker's repertoire are used (and possibly stored) separately. Yet, from this research, it is evident that the use of MIX enables students to refer to all parts of their experience, using the language elements with which they are most happy — namely English for academic jargon, MIX words for student life, and Cantonese for the remaining majority of their speech. Although purists may find the use of MIX deplorable, it evidently gives students maximum expressive potential, ranging within single utterances across their speech repertoire.

Towards a Theory of Code Choice

The studies reported in preceding chapters have examined various dimensions of code choice. "Code choice" is here given a broad interpretation following Scotton (1980 and 1983). It includes switching related to macro-sociolinguistic factors, code swaying and rhetorical choices. The psychological element of the level of conscious awareness and deliberateness in choosing a particular code has not been empirically examined, and in consequence cannot be treated further: however, it would merit investigation in subsequent studies.

A number of factors have been shown to correlate with code choice, including topic, social situation and the identity characteristics of the participants in Chapters 3 – 5. Code choice has also been shown (in Chapters 4 and 6) to express elements of the social relationship and produce rhetorical effects. Many of the other studies to which reference has been made support these statements. The two types of relationship can be expressed as follows:

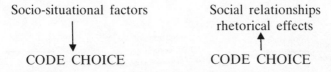

The model on the left encapsulates in a simplified form much of the underlying theory of macro- and micro-sociolinguistics, while that on the right crudely represents part of the social psychology of language model, and also the Gumperz and Austin school views of meaning in code choice.

The intention of the remainder of this section is to attempt the integration of these two perspectives into a single theoretical model. Similar attempts have been made by Giles, Smith & Robinson (1980) and Scotton (1980 and 1983), and the model described here is influenced by this work, although there are a number of major differences.

Referring first to Chapter 2, a number of traditional macro-sociolinguistic elements were isolated which are crucial to a theory of code choice. One important set consisted of various *identity features* of the participants, their ethnicity and educational level (first study), and their age (probabilistic study). Another important element in the first study was the circumstance, or *social situation*. Finally, the *topic* proved important in both the probabilistic study in Chapter 2 and in the study of code swaying in Chapter 5. It is also necessary to repeat that it is the speaker's *perceptions* of these various factors that influence code choice. Clearly speakers cannot always have objective knowledge of the entire range of these factors. Rather they will have judgements of them, which are held with varying degrees of conviction, and with varying degrees of objective accuracy. Summarizing, we can posit the following perceived factors in code choice:

    social situation
    identity characteristics of participants
    topic

Two other groups of factors which are needed in the model also emerged in Chapter 2. The first was physical *setting* in time and place. It was postulated that this might best be viewed as exerting an indirect influence on code choice, through the mediation of perception of the factors just described. The model can thus be built up as follows in Figure 21.

The use of the term "influence" (rather than "correlate with") is speculative, but there is a sufficient accumulation of evidence from many other

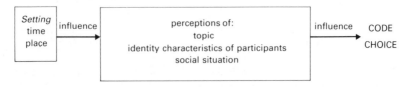

FIGURE 21

speech communities to make this interpretation not unreasonable (see Scotton & Ury, 1977; Gumperz, 1976; Sankoff, 1972). The nature of the influence upon code choice appears to be probabilistic rather than absolute as we have seen in the statistical studies. In Chapter 2 it was proposed that various elements within the perceived factors bias the speaker in varying degrees towards choosing one code rather than another. It was further suggested that these influences will accord on occasions, leading to relatively unambiguous pressure for a particular code choice, and conflict on other occasions, leaving the appropriate choice far less constrained. Much of the time the influence will be weighted more or less to various of the code choices.

The other group of factors which were needed in the model were those described in Chapter 3 as "external" factors. These include the language competences of the participants, and imposed regulations. Clearly, to address listeners in a language or code that they do not understand will not promote effective communication, although this can occur (see Scotton, 1983). Examples of imposed regulations are the Hong Kong Official Languages Ordinance, and the imposition of English as the instructional medium at the University of Hong Kong which explained many uses of English as described in Chapter 2. There is a link between regulations and the perceived factors, inasmuch as the former are often tied to particular factors: thus English is imposed upon the social situation "university instruction".

Two types of psychological factor are also involved in code choice. One consists of long term attitudes towards codes and their speakers. For example, the attitudes towards the use of MIX, Cantonese and English disclosed in Chapter 6 might well influence code choice. Such attitudes might derive from the history, experiences and socio-political situation of the group. However, once more the perceived factors would play a role — for example, attitudes towards using English with Westerners would differ from attitudes towards using English with Chinese: the attitudes are linked to the identity factor "ethnicity". The second type of psychological factor is the speaker's state of mind at the moment of speaking. Such psychological states as anxiety and anger are well documented as influencing code choice (see Giles & Powesland, 1975: 119–20). Psychological state may also be affected by the time or place.

The enlarged model is shown in Figure 22.

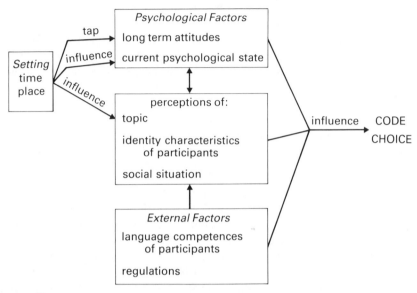

FIGURE 22

If we return to the central problem outlined at the beginning of this section, it is necessary to find some way of integrating the two models. A clue may come from the social meaning, and the elements of the social relationship which are affected by code choice. As Ryan (1979) indicates, these are frequently along the power/prestige and solidarity paradigms. However, the perceived factors can *also* affect social relationships directly. The effects of the three categories of factors are all documented. Taking first "identity characteristics", one could cite the work of Goffman (1971). An example from African societies is the prestige/power often accorded to old age; by contrast persons of peer age in many societies tend to a predisposition of solidarity unless other factors intervene. Again, the "social situation" can affect the social relationship (Lindesmith & Strauss, 1967: 281–82). For instance, the classroom instruction situation may accentuate the power element in a teacher-student relationship, while having lunch together may increase solidarity. Goffman (1971) also gives evidence for the part played by "topic" in social relationships. This enables us to link up the two models as shown in Figure 23. Another line of approach which will enable us to build up the integrated model is to ask the question — what is the mechanism by which code choice can affect social relationships? Certainly very important in this are the identity associations of the code.

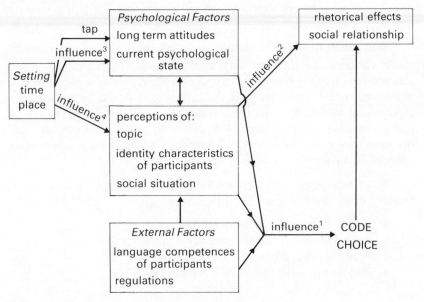

FIGURE 23

The participants in a verbal interaction have identity features of the sociodemographic type already discussed. Participants may not know each other well, and desire to explore the possibility of furthering the social relationship. In these cases the participants will need to reveal and present themselves (often in a favourable light), and to probe each other's identity (Berger, 1979). Code choice can be used to reveal various aspects of the speaker's identity. Scotton (1976), for example, speaks of the difficulty of deciding when to reveal one's knowledge of a code which is normally associated with a high level of education — too early, and one might appear immodest; too late, and the participants may have made (and acted upon) false judgements of one's identity and status. At this early stage speakers may reveal the sociopolitical belief element of their identity by careful choice of code (Giles & Powesland, 1975: 75 ff). To reveal elements of one's identity may also fulfil personal as well as social needs. Speakers may need to express their identity in this way, in order to maintain their self-image. It is not unheard of for speakers to use code choices to claim identity characteristics which they lack in reality. Le Page (1978) would say that speakers adopt sociolinguistic speech markers which express their aspirations toward and identification with social groups, including some to which they do not belong. He calls this an "act of identity" and writes: "Each speech act is an anouncement: 'to this extent I wish to be thought of as my own man, to this extent like A, to this extent like B, to this extent like C . . .' and so on."

While the expression of identity *per se* is important, code choices which mark elements of identity may also be used to shape the ongoing relationship. Initially one might expect that the choice of a code which was associated with identity features that are *shared* would be an attempt to close social distance, to increase solidarity, and that code choices that emphasize *differences* in identity would be an attempt to increase social distance, to alienate the hearer. While there is truth in this assumption, it is probably oversimplified (Giles & Smith, 1979).

If A when speaking to B chooses a code which marks a specific identity feature, there are four possible solutions:

1. A and B have the identity feature
2. neither A nor B has the identity feature
3. A has the feature but B does not
4. A does not have the feature but B does.

	A	B
1.	+	+
2.	−	−
3.	+	−
4.	−	+

+ = has the identity feature
− = does not have the identity feature

1. Where both A and B have the identity feature, one can normally assume that the choice of code to emphasize something shared is an attempt to close social distance. This in turn may serve to strengthen an argument, improve a sales pitch, etc. Giles & Powesland (1975) in their discussion of accommodation theory present strong evidence in favour of such a conclusion.

2. The choice of a code marking an identity feature that neither participant possesses can have at least two effects, depending on the situation. If A has open to him options which may alienate B by emphasizing a difference between them, then this may be a "neutral" choice to avoid offence; see Scotton (1976) for many examples. On the other hand, if A has open only other choices which emphasize common identity features, then the choice of another code may be an attempt to create social distance.

3. Where A has the feature and B does not, to emphasize this difference is likely to be an attempt to distance B. Alternatively it may be flattery — assigning B a favourable identity feature that he/she does not in fact have.

Sometimes a speaker can increase attraction by emphasizing an identity feature that is not shared; for example, if the topic and social situation are appropriate, emphasis on one's sex may prove attractive to members of the opposite sex; a slight foreign accent with exotic connotations may also be attractive.

4. Where A uses a code that is associated with an identity feature that s/he lacks, but B, the interlocutor *has*, then this is often an attempt to close social distance: however, such claims can be unacceptable to B — see Parkin (1974: 194–95), and Giles & Smith (1979).

Returning now to the model, and integrating these insights, we have seen that speakers can, by their code choice, accentuate or play down the effects upon the social relationship of the *identity features* of the participants. Speakers by their code choices can also emphasize or over-ride the effects of elements of the *social situation* upon social relationships – Scotton (1980) speaks convincingly of the person in authority who initially emphasizes the formal features of the situation, but once respect is established, is prepared to relax, and choose codes which emphasize less formal aspects. The mechanism, then, can be seen as one in which the various, *already existing influences of social situation and the identity of the participants upon the social relationship, are manipulated by choosing particular codes*: these codes can accentuate or play down these influences because of associations between codes and elements of these factors (essentially the same elements that operate along the "influence[1]" line of the model). An analogy would be to see the "influence[2]" arrow of the model as a spectrum of effects that the social situation and the identity of participants (and possibly also the topic) have upon the social relationship. Code choice dims or strengthens certain parts of that spectrum, thus manipulating the effects that social situation and identity features have upon the social relationship. At a higher level of abstraction, in this model code choice itself is seen as a way of negotiating social relationships, using existing social forces as a mechanism. The psychological factors of long term attitudes and current psychological state will also obviously affect the social relationship.

Rhetorical effects are obtained in a similar fashion. Once the code choice is established, the deliberate over-riding of the choice in a particular element of the discourse highlights this element and makes it salient, thus contributing towards the desired effect. The development of the model thus far is summarized in Figure 24.

An interesting case where a particular identity feature was strongly marked to assert solidarity (and perhaps also prestige) occurred in the first

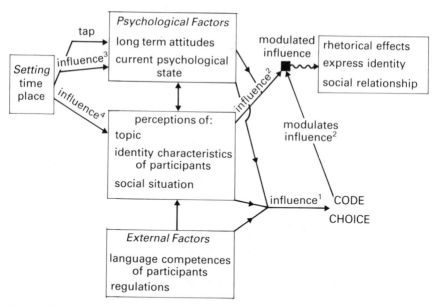

FIGURE 24

study in Chapter 2. We have noted a very strong social norm opposing the use of spoken English among Chinese, since this is viewed as a denial of Chinese ethnicity. Nevertheless, in one exceptional case two young Chinese women held an entire conversation in English. The social situation assisted them, in that it was a private circumstance, where outside social pressure was felt less strongly. The main factor appears to have been that the two women had attended a highly westernized élite school in which English is used among students. The former friends had subsequently gone their different ways. By violating the strong norm in favour of Chinese, and using English, the language of their school experience, they were probably strongly emphasizing this shared identity characteristic and asserting solidarity. This type of experience, when friends from a former period meet and slip back into the language behaviour of that period, is not uncommon. This model can accept and explain such behaviour.

The final consideration in the model is one of degree rather than design. We have spoken here, and in Chapter 2, of a varying degree of pressure towards the selection of a specific code or codes. (When the pressure is held constant, and a particular code is chosen repeatedly, this can also develop a form of inertia, which exerts in turn additional pressure.) Essentially, to use Scotton's (1980 and 1983) terminology, the greater the pressure to use a particular code, the less meaningful or

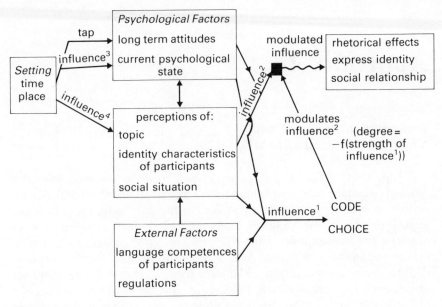

FIGURE 25

"marked" is it to use that code, and the more meaningful or "marked" to reject the pressure and choose another code. In other words, the strength of a code choice in influencing the social relationship, or in obtaining a rhetorical effect, is a negative (or reverse) function of the strength of the pressure towards that particular code choice. This final element completes the model in Figure 25.

It is certainly possible to suggest further elaborations of the model, including a feedback arrow from the right hand box to the psychological factors. Scotton would also probably wish to see a feedback arrow into the perceived factors box, since she would regard most of these perceptions as in some sense negotiable. Such additions would be rather speculative, however.

The model is a dynamic one, in which social relations are continually negotiated and the identity characteristics of the participants are expressed by code choices. As such, this model should be seen as forming part of a yet broader model of communicative competence (Hymes, 1972). The model may help researchers, by serving as a framework for the investigation and description of code choice behaviour. Although there are inevitably omissions and errors, it may serve as a step towards a more complete version.

Appendix 1

Transcription[1] of Tape 256 of
A Student Conversation in MIX

Tape 256 is a recording of a conversation between four students in the room of one of them. A and D are History majors, B and C are Philosophy majors. A is a "fresher" recently arrived at the university, the others are second or third year students. The numbered lines in what follows comprise the transcription of the conversation. The Cantonese element is transcribed in the widely used Yale Romanization. This Romanization is slightly idealized on occasions. The main focus of attention, the elements of English origin, are in square brackets [ ] if the word does not appear to conform entirely to the Cantonese phonological system, or alternatively in slashes / / if the pronunciation of the element has been entirely assimilated to Cantonese phonology (pure R. P. pronunciation did not occur). There are occasional footnotes which explain why certain words were not regarded as conforming to Cantonese phonology. Beneath the transcription is a loose English translation which attempts to retain some of the flavour of the original. English elements in the translation which also occur in the original conversation are italicized. A commentary indicating some salient characteristics of the speech behaviour follows the transcription.

1. D.   haih m̀h haih wán go /⌐kɛ ˌsi/ làih góng
         Are they looking for a *guest* to come and talk on that
2.   gó go   taih muhk a.
                  topic?
3. B.   haih a. wán a   [fa: ðə k'ɔlɪns] làih góng
         Yes.   They asked *Father Collins*   to talk on
4.   [⌐a pˡɔ ʂən] a. chòh kéuih la. gáng haih.
         abortion.   Let's grill him!   Really!
5. C.   Fai sih a. m̀h jì haih m̀hhaih hóu chíh seuhngchi
         Don't bother.   I don't know if it will be like last time.

136

6.   gám, yáuh yéh tái. dím jì dōu móuh.
               something to see.   Finally nothing.

7. A.   wai, néih hóu dò sìh dōu mēyéh ge wo.
               Hey, you often   whotsit (can't think of word).

8.   hóu dō sìh   [wan a wei] ge wo.   [p'ei t̯ruan]
               you   often   *run away* you say. *Play*   *truant*

9.   wo néih, haih m̀hhaih a?
               you say,   right?

10. B.   [p'ei truan]?
               play truant?

11. C+D. síu sih la!
               No big deal! (literally – a little thing)

12. B.   gēng yàhn jūk néih   ⌐ mē
               Afraid of people catching you?   │

13. D.   └ yau jih yúen hōi chi
                                  Ever since he was
                                  at kindergarten

14.   dou yih gā.
               he has been the same.

15. A.   síu sih haih m̀hhaih giu jouh [li t'ʋ fiŋ] a
               Does 'síu sih' mean *little thing*?

16. B.   néih m̀h ji la.   gó di [⌐lɛk⌐ ts'œ ˌla]
               You don't know. Those   *lecturers*

17.   gám làhm sihn m̀h pa ge. móuh yàhn dím méng
               are so nice   you needn't be frightened. Not one of those

18.   ge gó dî [⌐lɛk⌐ ts'œ ˌraᴗa
               lecturers takes a register.

19. A.   móuh [⌐w ɔu ⌐k'ɔ:] ge mē, néihdeih, móuh
               No   *roll call*   eh? You guys, no

20.   [⌐wɔu `k'ɔ:] ge mē
               roll   *call*   eh?

21. B.   gáng móuh lā. [rɔu] mēyeh /⌐k'ɔ/āa?
               Of course there isn't. What are you talking about, *roll call*

22. D.   néih gwu juhng haih jūng hohk a. [⌐rɔu –k'ɔ:] wo.
               You think you're still at secondary school. *Roll call* you say.

23. A.   wei néih seung tòhng   juhng yáuh móuh hóu
               Hey, when you go to classes   do you *day dream*

24.   chi jūng hohk gám [tˡɛi tr̥rimiŋ] aa?
                 like in secondary school?

25.   hái douh yàuh ┌ fauh a?
                 Do you day   │ dream there?

26. D.   └ yáuh la tai kéuih ┌ go yéuhg
                                   Yes!   Like │ him.

27. B. or C.   ├ gáng haih yáuh la
                                                    │ Of course we do.

28. B. or C.   └ haih a
                                                      Yes.

29. C.   (inaudible)

30. D.   yàuh kèih séuhng /_fi ⁻lo/ tim!
                 Especially when you do *philo*sophy!

31. B   /_fi⁻lo/   kéuih ngap   néih   yauh   m̀hjī kéuih
                In *philo*sophy he rabbits on, you never know what

32.   góng mátyéh hah! ┌ kéuih yauh hái douh . . .
                 he is talking about! │ When he talks . . .

33. A.   └ Wei, hóu chíh yàhn deih wah
                                   Hey, it seems that everyone says,

34.   mātyéh go wo duhk /_fi ⁻lo/ lē, [ɪn sɜ:tʃˈəfˡ
                 how to put it, that in studying *philo*sophy, you are *in search*
                 of

35.   sœ:tˈənt'i] gwo, gám néih [sœts'] dóu dī
                 certainty,   so what have you *search*ed

36.   mēyéh sîn a?
                 out?

37. D.   ngóhdeih   [sœts'] dóu   [ɛpˡ sœtˡ ti ,t'i:]. (laughter)
                 We have   *search*ed out *absurdity*.

38. A.   [psœtˡ ti t'i]
                 Absurdity.

39. C.   ah, haih a, hah go laih baai wah, /_fi⁻lo/
                 Oh yes,   next week   they say, *philo*sophy

40.   gáau [⁻kˡɛm]², néih heui m̀hheui a?
                 is organizing a *camp*,   are you going?

41. D.   /_fi⁻lo/ gáau   [k'ɛm]   ⌐ mē?
             *Philo*sophy is organizing a *camp*, | hey?
42. B.   └ hah go yuht.
                                                        Next month.

43. C.   Hah go yuht mē?
             Next month, hey?

44. B.   hah go yuht [⁻k'ɛm ˌp'iŋ] ngóh gáng haih   ⌐ heui lā . . .
             (inaudible) |
             Next month *camping*,   I am definitely | going.
45. C.   └ mēyeh
                                                            What's

46.   [mɔrisan haus⎵ aa.
             this *Morrison* ⌐ *House* place?
             (inaudible) |
47. B.   . . . .[mɔrɪsan hausi] léuhng   yaht ā ma.
                             Morrison House   for two   days.

48.   ngóh heui chím jó meng a, ngóh [sain]³ jó la.
             I have been to sign up,   I have *sign*ed.

49. A.   wai,   hóu chíh juhng yáuh   [_k'ä ⁻nu] pàh wa.
             Hey, it seems they have   *canoe*ing, so I have heard.

50. D.   /_k'a ⁻nu/
             *Canoe*ing

51. C.   mē yéh /_k'a⁻nu/ a.
             What *canoe*?

52. B.   m̀hhaih gwaa. bîn douh yáuh deih fōng
             No way!   Where is there a place for you

53.   béi néih pàh /_k'a⁻ nu/ a   ⌐ daaih lóu?
             to go   *canoe*ing | chum?
54. A.   └ yáuh!
                                            There is!

55. B.   seuhngbihn gódouh, bîn   yáuh dāk pàh à,
             Up   there,   how can you go boating,

56.   daaih lóu?
             chum?

57. D.   pàh syuh jauh yáuh.
             You can climb trees (pun on pàh – climb/row).

58. C.   nî yeung jauh hauh hei la, jàn haih.
         This type I really can't manage.

59. B.   bāt gwo tèng góng wah [⁻mɔ⁻ri⁻san ⁻hau ,si] a,
         But I have heard that   *Morrison*   *House*

60.   hóu jeng ge wo. yauh [⁻ɛ:–k'ɔn ⁻t¹i , ʃan]   ge wo.
         is great.   There's [*air-condition*ing   they say.

61. C.   [⁻ɛ: –k'ɔn ⁻t¹i ,ʃan]àah
                                    Air-conditioning!

62. B.   yauh sihng wo.
         And more they say.

63. A.   [⁻ɛ: –k'ɔn ⁻t¹i ,ʃan]àh?
         Air-conditioning!

64. B.   bāt gwo yìh gā haih láahng tīn jē, sèui joih.
         But now its   winter (literally cool weather), unfortunately.

65. C.   gám ['k'ɔu] sái māt [⁻ɛ] m̀h [⁻ɛ] a? nik jó heui
         Seeing it is so *cold*, what's the use of *air-condition*ing. If they
         take

66.   dōu, móuh só waih lā.
         it away, it doesn't matter.

67. B.   iauh haih lā, sàai jó ā ma.
         Exactly,   it is wasted.

68. C.   yih sahp ngàhm, haih m̀hhaih a.
         twenty   dollars,   right?

69. B.   haih la, [⁻t'wᵉen ⁻t'i ⁻p¹ak¹ ,si] a.
         Yes,   *twenty*   *bucks*.

70. C.   [⁻t'wᵉen ⁻t'i ⁻p¹ak ,si]
         Twenty bucks.

71. B.   m̀hhaih wo, tèng góng wah jíhaih hóyíh
         No,   I've heard that there's only room

72.   yùhng naahp [t'ᵉen t'u t'wᵉen t'i p'ip'œu]
         for   *ten to twenty people*.

73.   ge ja wo, gàm chi go [⁻k'ɛm,p'iŋ].
         or so on this *camping* (trip).

74. A.   [sɔu smɔ:]
         So small!

75. B.   jān ga.
            Really!

76. A.   [riᵛli]
            Really

77. B.   [rɪəli], gáng haih [rɪəli] lā!
            Really, of course *really*!

78. C.   néih hah jau yáuh móuh séung tòhng a?
            Did you go to class this afternoon?

79. A.   (in ði aft'œ nun ju min]
            In   the   afternoon   you mean?

80. C. ⌐ gám gánghaih lā
            Of course.

81. B. ⌐ [ɔf¹ kɔs]
            Of course.

82. A.   [sœtənli]
            Certainly.

83. C.   [sɜ:tənli]
            Certainly.

84. D.   wei, néihdeih /_fi⁻lo/ ge,   yáuh géi dò go
            Hey,   you people who do *philo*sophy, how many

85.   /⌐t'ju ‚t'a/ le?
            tutors are there?

86. C.   /_fi ⁻lo/₍c₎
            *Philo*sophy . . .

87. B.   /_fi⁻lo ⁻t'ju ‚t'a/₍c₎ àh? /⌐t'ju ‚t'a/ hóudō a.
            *Philo*sophy   tutors?   There are lots of *tutors*.

88. C. ⌐ yáuh [⌐p'at¹ ⁻t'aim]⁴, yáuh [_fu ⁻t'aim]⁴
            There are *part-time*,   there are *full-time*,

89. ?   ⌐ (inaudible)

90. B.   yáuh [⌐p'at¹ ⁻t'aim]⁴, yáuh [_fu ⁻t'aim]⁴
            There are   *part-time*, there are *full-time*,

91.   haih m̀hhaih ā? yauh yáuh [lɛk¹tsrœ]
            right?   Also there are *lecturers*

92.   jouh   /⌐t'ju ‚t'a /
            acting as   *tutors*

93. A.   yáuh géidò go [mɛi], yáuh géidò go
            How many *males* are there, and   how many

94.　　　[fimɛiu] a?
　　　　　females are there?

95.　B.　[fimɛil]áh?　⌈[ɛn . . . niᵘl . . . ɛn ai el] móuh.
　　　　　Females?　│　*N . . . Nil . . . N . . . I . . . L none.*
96.　C.　　　　　　　└ hóu chíh móuh a.
　　　　　　　　　　　It seems there are none.

97.　D.　móuh.
　　　　　None.

98.　C.　móuh wo,　⌈ chyùhnbouh [mɛioᵘ]
　　　　　None you say,　│ entirely　*male.*
99.　B.　　　　　　　└ [⎺hi – stri] yáuh móuh ga?
　　　　　　　　　　　Are there any in *History?*

100.　A.　ngóhdeih go [⎺hi –stri], eh . . .　　[ði ɔuni wan]
　　　　　Our *History* department, eh　(*the*) *only one.*

101.　dāk yāt go la, dāk yāt go [ða wan ɛn ou ni wan]
　　　　Only one,　　　only one　*the one and only one.*

102.　B.　dou hóu gwo /⎺fi _lo/ ā.　　móuh! jànhaih
　　　　　Still better than *Philo*sophy. None! Really

103.　géi chāam a.
　　　　dreadful.

104.　A.　néih yáuhmóuh [t'ɛik¹ ts'ainis] ga néih?
　　　　　Do you　　　*take Chinese*　　you?

105.　B.　ngóh mēyéh móuh [t'ɛik¹ ts'ainis] a.　⌈ léuhng fò
　　　　　Of course I　　*take Chinese*　　│ I *take* two
106.　D.　　　　　　　　　　　　　　　　　　└ (inaudible)

107.　B.　[tɛik¹] saai. [ts'ainis] tùhng [ts'ainis ⎺hi–stri]
　　　　　courses.　　*Chinese*　and　*Chinese History.*

108.　C.　/⎺t'u ⎺ko ˌsi/ haih m̀hhaih a?
　　　　　Two courses　right?

109.　B.　gáng haih lā.
　　　　　Of course.

110.　C.　gám dîm a, jikhaih . . .
　　　　　What then, I mean . . .

111.　B.　dîm a, ngóh yāt jahngāan jauh yiu heui
　　　　　What?　　　Later I'll go to the

112.　[⎺sp'ɔt¹ ⎺sɛn ˌt'a]⁵ . . . (inaudible) ge la.
　　　　Sports Centre.

113. C.   néih m̀h séung tòhng?
          You are not going to class?

114. B.   gánghaih m̀hséung lā.
          Of course not!

115. A.   wei, gó go [⁻sp'ɔt¹ ⁻sɛn ‚t'a lɔu k'ɛi] hái
          Hey,   that   Sports Centre   is located

116.   bîn douh, [lɔuk'ɛisən] hái bîn a?
          where,   what is its location?

117. B.   [lɔuk'ɛiscœn lɔuk'ɛiscœn] a, hái [‚siŋ ⁻tsɔn ‚siŋ ⁻tsɔns
          location, location   opposite St. John's   St. John's

118.   kɔlɪts] deui mihn.
          College.

119. A.   [siŋ kɔ]
          Saint Co. . ?

120. B.   jikhaih /siŋ ⁻tson/ a, /–ho/ a, [sein̯'d ʒɔns
          I mean St. John's hall, opposite Saint John's,

121.   sein̯'d ʒɔns k'ɔlɪts] deuimihn.
          Saint John's   College

122. A.   jikhaih [sein tsɔn] deuimihn.
          That is opposite Saint John's

123. B.   haih la, móuh cho la. néih, néih m̀hhaih /‚a⁻fɛi
          Yes,   that's right.   You, you are not an Affiliated
          Member

124.   ‚siŋ ⁻tson/ ge mē?
          of St. John's?

125. A.   ngóh m̀hhaih, ngóh, ngóh haih mēyéh ga, ngóh
          No I'm not,   I,   what am I?   I

126.   haih   ⌈ /‚ou ‒ho/   ge /‚a ⁻fei/ làih ge.
          am an   │ Old Halls Affiliated Member.

127. C. or D.   ⌊ [‚ou ‒hɔs]
                      Old Halls.

128. B.   m̀h gwaai dāk jì lā.
          No wonder!

129. A.   néih yáuh móuh jyuh [hɔstɔuʷ] a, néih?
          Do you live in a   hostel,   you?

130. D.   móuh a, mouh.
          No, no.

131. C.   /_a ⁻fɛi/ nē?
            Affiliated then?

132. D.   kéuih m̀hbéi ngóh ā la.   ⌈ ngóh búnlòih yíhgîng
            They would let me.   │ I have already applied.

133..   sāanchíng jó ge la. B. or C.   ⌊ néih móuh /_a ⁻fɛi / àh?
                                             You are not *affiliated*?

134. B. or C.   (inaudible) /_a⁻fɛi/ a. néih móuh /_a ⁻fɛi/ àh?
                . . .   *affiliated.*   You are not *affiliated*?

135. D.   si gwo ge, [ɔu hɔs] ge, dōu haih.
            I used to be,   *Old Halls,* too.

136. C.   dōu haih /⌐ou –ho/.
            Old Halls too.

137. B.   dōu haih /⌐ou –ho ˏsi/, tàam /⌐ou –ho ˏsi/
            Old Halls too,   what do you like about

138.   mēyéh hóu a?
            Old Halls?

139. D.   e –   béi gaau,   hó nàhng mēyéh lā, nàahm
            Er there are more,   so to speak,   male

140.   néuih sàng . . . (laughter)
            and female students.

141. B.   m̀h haih gwa.
            I guess not.

142. C.   hóu jaahp léh.
            Lots of complications!

143. B.   m̀h haih wo, /_siŋ ⁻tson ˏsi/   ⌈ /_siŋ ⁻tsɔn ˏsi/
            No,   *St. John's*   │ *St. John's*

144. C.   ⌊ [siŋ tsɔns] dōu haih.
                                                 St. John's is also.

145. B.   dōu haih /⌐k'ou/, jik haih dōu haih /⌐k'ou–ɛt/
            is also   *co–,*   that is, it is also   *co-ed.*

146.   ge wo.

147. D.   [t'u fa awɛi fɔm sku]   ⌈ lā! (laughs)
            Too far away from school!   │

148. B.   ⌊ [t'u fa] haih la.
                                                 Yes, *too far.*

149. B.   e . . . yàhndeih hóu dò, jauhhaih tàam kéuih
                 Er . . . lots of people like it because it is

150.   yúhn dī, yauh jihng, jauhhaih m̀hhaih dím
                 further, so quiet,   if not why do so

151.   wúih gam do nàahmjái jūngyi yahp /_siŋ ⁻tson/
                            many guys   like to get into   *St. John*'s?

152..   ⌈ ā
153. D.   ⌊ m̀h jàn   ah, m̀h gau [–ɔu ⁻hɔs] gám jehng ge.
                 That is not true, it is not as quiet as *Old Halls*.

154. B.   [sein tsɔns] sàn ge wo, daaih wo.
                 St. John's is new,   and big.

155. C.   géisìh dáyùhn bō a, néih daaihyeuk yuhbeih?
                 When do you finish your game, when do you expect,
                 approximately?

156. B.   ngóhdeih? ngóhdeih a – sàam dím léhng ⌈ lā
                 Us?   We, er,   after three o'clock │

157. C.   ⌊ sàam
                                                             After

158.   dìm léhng àh? gām heui /⁻la:i/gei dāng néih ā.
                 three o'clock eh?   Then I'll wait for you at the *li*brary eh?

159. B.   /_la:i/gei? waahkjé fàan/⁻la:i/gei,
                 The *li*brary?   Maybe   I'll go to the *li*brary,

160.   waahkjé m̀hfàan ge wo.
                 maybe not.

161. C.   waahkjé fàan waahkjé m̀hfàan àh?
                 Maybe you'll go, maybe not?

162. D.   [⁻spɔt¹⁻sɛn,t'a] gèisìh [klɘus] ga?
                 What time does the *Sports Centre close*?

163. B.   [⁻spɔt ⁻sɛn ‚t'a:] ?   hóuchíh haih tìngyaht [klɔus]
                 The *Sports Centre*?   It seems to me it is *close*d tomorrow,

164.   ge wo, hóuchih. ngóh m̀hjî wo, ngóh m̀hjî
                 it seems.   I don't know,   I don't know

165.   [ɛk¹sɛk¹li] géi do dím, jauh ngóh nám haih
                 exactly   what time, but   I   think it is

166.   [ɘ p'ɔk¹ si mœt¹li] baat dím léhng lā,   gáu dím lā.
                 approximately   eight something, or nine.

167. C.   wàh, gam yeh.
                 Wow,   so late.

Commentary on tape 256

Line

1. *Phonology*: the word "guest" has undergone extensive phonological modification to fit the MIX/Cantonese system, including
   the loss of final /–t#/, the addition of final /–i#/, and the
   introduction of tone.

6. *Motives for code choice*: student A clearly cannot retrieve from
   memory an appropriate Cantonese word, so he uses two English
   items "run away" and "play truant". This is an example of how the
   non-availability of a word can trigger a conscious code-switch (see
   Chapter 4).

15. *Motives for code choice*: student A has previously been derided for
    carrying over school norms to the university situation. The highly
    marked introduction of "little thing" may be a bid to re-establish
    A's status (c.f. Scotton, 1983).

21. *Grammar*: the English element "roll call" is divided in accordance
    with the Cantonese grammatical pattern. See also the comment on
    line 65.

30. *Lexis/Code choice*: /_fi⁻lo/ is a good example of a highly integrated
    item. It is clear from the paralinguistic evidence in many occur-
    rences on this tape that this term is used increasingly as part of the
    discourse.

34. *Motives for code choice*: this is probably an example of a conscious
    switch in order to quote an exact form of words (see Chapter 4).

37. *Motives for code choice*: the choice of the English word "absur-
    dity" here is clearly conscious, and is for humorous effect.

40. *Phonology*: the violation of Cantonese phonotactics in the case of
    "camp" (found in other MIX words) has clearly not prevented this
    word from being integrated in the MIX discourse.

48. *Motives for code choice*: an example of "bilingual echoing", which,
    from the paralinguistic clues, is probably emphatic.

65. *General*: what sounds like a Cantonese sentence has English
    content words. Along with the high level of phonological assimila-
    tion, the [⁻ɛ] derived from "air" is repeated to fit the Cantonese
    syntax.

69. *Lexis*: the word bāk sìh is also used elsewhere in Hong Kong.

76. *Motives for code choice*: the English word "really" may have been
    used either for emphasis, or as an unsuccessful ploy (see line 77) to
    avoid conflict with B. In the latter case it may have been an

attempt to express doubt about B's statement without repeating his exact (Chinese) words.

87. *General*: in this line and in those that follow there are a number of utterances which sound like Cantonese, yet most or all of their content words are English, with some violations of Cantonese phonotactics (see Chapter 3).

104. *Semantics*: "Chinese" is an example of the use of an English lexical item to refer to a University subject — i.e. semantic specialization (see Chapter 3). The Chinese equivalent of "Chinese" is, of course, readily available.

112. *Phonology*: "Sports Centre" here is assigned tone, and is totally assimilated to Cantonese phonology, except that the initial English /#sp–/ cluster is retained intact. This is a clear example of "systematic retention" and evidence of the intermediate MIX phonological system.

120. *Motives for code choice*: since A does not know the MIX form of "St. John's College" — /₋siŋ⁻tson/, B uses a more standard English pronunciation (line 121). An example of a MIX→English switch.

126ff. *Phonology*: instability in MIX forms is illustrated by three variants of the pronunciation of "Old Halls": /₋ou –ho/, [₋ɔu –hɔs] and /⌐ou –hoˎsi/.

158. *Lexis*: /⌐laːi -kɛi/ "library" is an example of a loan blend.

165–6. *Motivation for code choice*: it is hard to conceive of any motivation for the use of "exactly" and "approximately" in English (Cantonese equivalents are readily available) other than a desire to continue to mix.

Notes to Appendix 1

1. I should like to thank Peter Barnes for help with transcribing elements of English Origin, and Irina Lau for help with transcribing Cantonese.
2. Although individual segmentals are Cantonese, the sequence [–ɛm#] is not in accord with Cantonese phonotactics. Other examples follow.
3. Although individual segmentals are Cantonese, the sequence [–ain#] is not in accord with Cantonese phonotactics.
4. Although individual segmentals are Cantonese, the sequence [–aim#] is not in accord with Cantonese phonotactics.
5. Although individual segmentals are Cantonese, the sequence [#sp–] does not occur in Cantonese.

Appendix 2

Rating Sheets from the Matched Guise Study

The example given here is the bilingual version. The monolingual version was identical except that the Chinese was omitted. The subjects were provided with three copies of the first sheet, one for each voice.

講 者

SPEAKER

你 對 說 話 的 人 一 般 觀 念 如 何

What is your general impression of the speaker? 你 認為, 為 講 者 是

Do you think the speaker is 你 認 為

大方　総不

01. helpful 樂於 助人

02. well mannered and polite 溫 文 有禮

03. friendly 友善

04. successful 成功

05. kind 善良

06. knowledgeable 博學 的

07. good looking 像 表 出 眾

08. understanding 善解 人 意

09. ambitious 有 雄心 壯志

Item	very much so	1	2	3	4	5	6	7	not at all
01. helpful		1	2	3	4	5	6	7	
02. well mannered and polite		1	2	3	4	5	6	7	
03. friendly		1	2	3	4	5	6	7	
04. successful		1	2	3	4	5	6	7	
05. kind		1	2	3	4	5	6	7	
06. knowledgeable		1	2	3	4	5	6	7	
07. good looking		1	2	3	4	5	6	7	
08. understanding		1	2	3	4	5	6	7	
09. ambitious		1	2	3	4	5	6	7	

To what extent do you think the speaker is

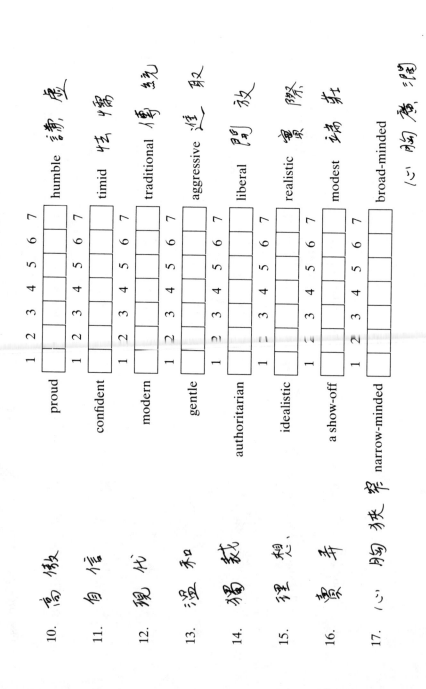

No.	Left	1	2	3	4	5	6	7	Right
10.	proud	1	2	3	4	5	6	7	humble
11.	confident	1	2	3	4	5	6	7	timid
12.	modern	1	2	3	4	5	6	7	traditional
13.	gentle	1	2	3	4	5	6	7	aggressive
14.	authoritarian	1	2	3	4	5	6	7	liberal
15.	idealistic	1	2	3	4	5	6	7	realistic
16.	a show-off	1	2	3	4	5	6	7	modest
17.	narrow-minded	1	2	3	4	5	6	7	broad-minded

請按以下之特點評定該講者

Please score the speaker on these features

18. clothes: 衣著

時尚 fashionable   1   2   3   4   5   6   7   不合時尚 unfashionable

沒有名氣

19. school: 學校

unknown   1   2   3   4   5   6   7   很有名氣 famous

20. cultural orientation: 文化認同

中國 Chinese   1   2   3   4   5   6   7   西方 Western

Please provide the following information about yourself (your name is not necessary).

Sex: M/F (Please circle one)   Faculty:

Year 1 / 2 / 3 (Please circle one)

Subjects you study:

Name(s) of your secondary school(s):

Please tick one box:

During the experiment, how did you feel?

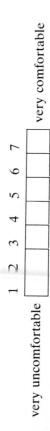

very uncomfortable   1 2 3 4 5 6 7   very comfortable

What is your cultural orientation?

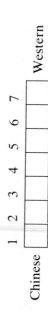

Chinese   1 2 3 4 5 6 7   Western

Thank you *very much* for your help!

Appendix 3

Statistical Model used in the Sociology of Language Study

Collett describes the statistical model used in Chapter 2 as follows:

"Write p_i for the probability that individual i speaks the mixture. This probability may be described by a linear logistic model where

$$P_i = \frac{e^{n_i}}{1 + e^{n_i}}$$

and n_i is a linear model containing the factors (independent variables). If this probability only depended on PSCHO, say, we should write

$$n_i = \mu + PSCHO_j$$

Where μ is an overall mean and $PSCHO_j$ is an effect due to the j'th school, $j = 1,2,3,4$. Similarly for the other combinations of variables.

The aim of the analysis is thus to find the best fitting linear logistic model which will indicate the variables which play an important role in determining which language is spoken.

To test the fit of various models we use a likelihood ratio statistic, called the *deviance*. When data is normal, the deviance is just the residual sum of squares. Here, the data is binomial (binary, in fact) and the deviance acts like a R.S.S. The deviance has a χ^2 distribution on a given number of degrees of freedom. To investigate the effect of various terms in the model, we compute the deviance and examine the change in deviance on including on excluding terms, (c.f. multiple regression). Values of a deviance near its d.f. indicate that the model is a good fit whilst differences in deviance are also χ^2."

Appendix 4

Statistical Model used in the Secular Linguistic Study

Bacon-Shone describes the statistical model that he used as follows:

"The proportions of each language in a situation were treated as random variables. This has the virtue of removing the problem of correlation between successive syllables [a major statistical problem for variable rules acknowledged by Sankoff & Laberge (1978)]. It was assumed that

$$v_1 = \log \frac{n_1}{n_3}, \quad v_2 = \log \frac{n_2}{n_3}$$

where n_1, n_2 and n_3 are the numbers of syllables of language 1, 2 and 3 in a given situation, and that a linear model could be used for the factors. Note that as the proportions add to one, we have only two free variables. Least square models were used for fitting the model. There was a problem of zero counts. This was avoided by adding ½ to all counts (this corresponds to a Dirichlet (½, ½, ½) prior in the Bayesian context). Also, in an attempt to take into account the greater accuracy when the syllable count is high, the observations were weighted by the total count. As we are now fitting a model linearly, we can use the SA 5 package to fit a general linear model and get the associated multivariate analysis of variance. However, as we have a large number of possible factors, let alone interactions, it is not possible to justify normality assumptions. Because of this the idea behind the analysis was not to choose statistically significant factors, but rather factors which are important in the sense of giving a large decrease in the sum of squares per parameter".

The following tables display the findings statistically, bearing in mind that:

$$v_1 = \left(\log \frac{n_e + \frac{1}{2}}{n_i + \frac{1}{2}} \right)$$

$$v_2 = \left(\log \frac{n_e + \frac{1}{2}}{n_c + \frac{1}{2}} \right)$$

e = other English syllables
i = "integrated" syllables
c = Cantonese

154

In these tables, and the plots derived from them, LS means are adjusted.

TABLE 11   *General Linear Models Procedure*
Least Square Means

| Group # | Groups | |
	V1 LS Mean	V2 LS Mean
3	0.64	−2.94
4	1.30	−1.74
5	0.25	−3.34
7	0.96	−3.00
10	0.41	−1.58
11	3.09	−2.53
12	2.33	−1.51
13	0.87	−3.98
14	0.72	−2.30
15	1.33	−3.36
16	1.47	−2.55
17	−0.69	−3.09
18	0.93	−1.65
19	0.05	−3.56
20	1.98	−1.69
21	0.40	−3.38
22	1.45	−2.16
23	0.92	−2.31
24	−0.53	−4.03
25	−2.51	−6.06
26	0.25	−2.08
27	1.11	−2.52
29	2.16	−1.04

TABLE 12

| | School | |
School Type	V1 LS Mean	V2 LS Mean
1	0.25	−2.77
2	1.02	−2.64
3	1.42	−2.23
4	0.59	−3.20

TABLE 13

| | Sex | |
	V1 LS Mean	V2 LS Mean
male 1	0.65	−2.93
female 2	0.99	−2.49

TABLE 14

Topic #	Topic V1 LS Mean	V2 LS Mean
1	1.75	−1.90
2	1.13	−2.45
3	0.30	−2.28
4	0.28	−2.80
5	0.76	−3.97
6	2.01	−1.80
7	0.26	−4.32
8	0.09	−2.18

Bibliography

AGHEYISI, R. N. 1977, Language Interlarding in the Speech of Nigerians. In P. F. A. KOTEY & H. DER-HOUSSIKIAN (eds), *Language and Linguistic Problems in Africa.* Columbia: Hornbeam Press, 97–110.

ANNAMALAI, E. 1971, Lexical Insertion in a mixed language, *Papers from the Seventh Regional Meeting of the Chicago Linguistic Society.* Chicago: Chicago Linguistic Society, 20–27.

BAETENS BEARDSMORE, H. 1982, *Bilingualism: Basic Principles.* Clevedon: Tieto.

BAKER, O. R. 1980, Categories of Code Switching in Hispanic Communities: Untangling the Terminology, *Working Papers in Sociolinguistics. 74–80.* Austin, Texas: Southwest Educational Development Laboratory.

BARCELONA, H. M. 1977, Language Usage and Preference Patterns of Filipino Bilinguals: An NMPC Survey. In E.M. PASCASIO *The Filipino Bilingual: Studies on Philippine Bilingualism and Bilingual Education.* Quezon City: Ateneo de Manila University Press. 64–71.

BAUMAN, R. & SHERZER, J. (eds) 1974, *Explorations in the Ethnography of Speaking.* Cambridge: Cambridge University Press.

BELL, R. (1976), *Sociolinguistics: Goals Approaches and Problems.* London: B. T. Batsford Ltd.

BERGER, C. 1979, Beyond Initial Interaction: Uncertainty, Understanding, and the Development of Interpersonal Relationships. In H. GILES & R. ST CLAIR (eds), *Language and Social Psychology.* 122–44.

BICKERTON, D. 1975, *Dynamics of a Creole System.* Cambridge: Cambridge University Press.

BLANC, H. 1968, The Israeli Koiné as an Emergent National Standard. In J. A. FISHMAN , C. A. FERGUSON & J. DAS GUPTA (eds), *Language Problems of Developing Nations.* 237–51.

BLOM, J. P. & GUMPERZ, J. J. 1972, Social Meaning in Linguistic Structure: Code-Switching in Norway. In J. J. GUMPERZ & D. HYMES (eds), *Directions in Sociolinguistics: The Ethnography of Communication.* 407–34. Also in J. J. GUMPERZ *Language in Social Groups: essays by John J. Gumperz.* 274–310.

BOLINGER, D. L. 1958, A theory of pitch accent in English. *Word* 14, 109–49.

BOND, M. H. & YANG, K. S. 1982, Ethnic Affirmation versus Cross-Cultural Accommodation: the Variable Impact of Questionnaire Language on Chinese Bilinguals in Hong Kong. *Journal of Cross Cultural Psychology*, 13, 2, 169–85.

BROWN, G. 1977, *Listening to Spoken English*. London: Longman.

BROWN, R. & GILMAN, A. 1960, The Pronouns of Power and Solidarity. In T. A. SEBEOK (ed.), *Style in Language*. Cambridge, Mass.: M.I.T. Press, 253–76. Also in P. P. GIGLIOLI, (ed.), *Language in Social Context: Selected Readings*. 252–82.

BYNON, T. 1977, *Historical Linguistics*. Cambridge: Cambridge University Press.

CEDERGREN, H. J. & SANKOFF, D. 1974, Variable rules: performance as a statistical reflection of competence. *Language*, 50, 2, 333–55.

CHAN Y. Y. 1968, *The spectral properties of Cantonese vowels: a comparison with English vowels*. Unpublished M. A. dissertation. University of Hong Kong.

CHAO, Y. R. 1968, *A Grammar of Spoken Chinese*. Berkeley: University of California Press.

CHENG, N. L., SHEK, K. C., TSE, K. K. & WONG, S. L. 1973, *At What Cost? Instruction through the English Medium in Hong Kong Schools*. Hong Kong: Language Centre, University of Hong Kong.

CHEUNG, Y. S. 1969, A Study of Even Tone and Change Tones in Cantonese as Spoken in Hong Kong. *Journal of the Institute of Chinese Studies*, 2, 1.

— 1972, *Studies on Cantonese as Spoken in Hong Kong*. Unpublished M. A. thesis, Chinese University of Hong Kong. (In Chinese).

CHIA, S. H. 1977, An Investigation into Language Use Among Secondary Four Pupils in Singapore – Pilot Project. In W. CREWE (ed.), *The English Language in Singapore*. 157–88.

CHUNG, S. N. 1975, *Morpheme and Syllable in Modern Standard Chinese*. Unpublished M. A. dissertation. Manchester: University of Manchester.

CLARK, H. H. & CLARK, E. V. 1977, *Psychology and Language: an Introduction to Psycholinguistics*. New York: Harcourt Brace Jovanovich.

CLYNE, M. G. 1967, *Transference and Triggering*. The Hague: Nijhoff.

COLTHARP, L. H. 1965, *The Tongue of the Tirilones: a Linguistic Study of a Criminal Argot*. Alabama: University of Alabama Press.

COOPER, R. L. 1969, How Can We Measure the Roles which a Bilingual's Languages Play in his Everyday Behaviour? In L. G. KELLY (ed.),

Description and Measurement of Bilingualism: an International Seminar, University of Moncton, June 6–14, 1967. 192–208.

COULTHARD, M. 1977, *An Introduction to Discourse Analysis*. London: Longman.

CREWE, W. 1977, *The English Language in Singapore*. Singapore: Eastern Universities Press.

DAS GUPTA, J. 1980, *Language conflict and national development; group politics and national language policy in India*. Berkeley: University of California Press.

DECAMP, D. 1971, Introduction: the Study of Pidgin and Creole Languages. In D. Hymes (ed.) *Pidginization and Creolization of Languages*. 13–39.

DIEBOLD, A. R. 1963, Code Switching in Greek-English Bilingual Speech, *Georgetown University Monograph Series on Language and Linguistics*, 15, 49–55.

DILLARD, J. L. 1972, *Black English: its History and Usage in the United States*. New York: Random House.

DITTMAR, N. 1976, *Sociolinguistics: a critical survey of theory and application*. London: Arnold.

EDWARDS, A. E. 1977, *Experimental Design in Psychological Research*. New York: Holt, Rinehart and Winston.

EDWARDS, J. 1979, *Language and Disadvantage*. London: Arnold.

ELÍAS-OLIVARES, L. 1976, *Ways of Speaking in a Chicago Community: A Sociolinguistic Approach*. Unpublished Ph. D. dissertation. University of Texas at Austin.

— 1979, Language use in a Chicano community: a sociolinguistic approach. In J. B. PRIDE (ed.), *Sociolinguistic Aspects of Language Learning and Teaching*. Oxford: Oxford University Press. 120–34.

ERVIN-TRIPP, S. M. 1964, An Analysis of the interaction of language, topic and listener. In J. J. GUMPERZ & D. HYMES (eds), *The Ethnography of Communication, special issue of American Anthropologist*, 66, 6, 86–102. Revised version in S. M. ERVIN-TRIPP (ed.) *Language Acquisition Communicative Choice, Essays by Susan M. Ervin-Tripp*. 239–61.

— 1967, An Issei Learns English. *The Journal of Social Issues*, 23, 2: 78–90. Also in S. M. ERVIN-TRIPP, *Language Acquisition and Communicative Choice, Essays by Susan M. Ervin-Tripp*. 62–77.

— 1969, Sociolinguistics. In L. BERKOWITZ (ed.), *Advances in Experimental Social Psychology*, vol. 4. New York: Academic Press, 93–107.

— 1973, *Language Acquisition and Communicative Choice. Essays by Susan M. Ervin-Tripp*. Selected and Introduced by A. S. Dil. Stanford: Stanford University Press.

FISHMAN, J. A. 1965, Who speaks what language to whom and when. *La Linguistique*, 2, 67–88.
— (ed.) 1968, *Readings in the Sociology of Language*. The Hague: Mouton.
— (ed.) 1971a, *Advances in the Sociology of Language*. 1. The Hague: Mouton.
— 1971b, First published as 'The Relationship between Micro- and Macro-Sociolinguistics in the Study of Who Speaks What Language to Whom and When' In J. A. FISHMAN et al., (eds), *Bilingualism in the Barrio*, 583–604. Also in J. PRIDE & J. HOLMES (eds), *Sociolinguistics*, 15–32, (slightly revised): and under title 'Domains and the Relationship between Micro- and Macro-Sociolinguistics' in J. GUMPERZ & D. HYMES *Directions in Sociolinguistics: Ethnography of Communication*, 435–53.
FISHMAN, J. A., COOPER, R. L. & MA, R., *et al.* 1971, *Bilingualism in the Barrio*. Bloomington and The Hague: Indiana University Press and Mouton.
FISHMAN, J. A., FERGUSON, C. A. & DAS GUPTA, J. (eds) 1968, *Language Problems of Developing Nations*. New York: Wiley.
FISHMAN, J. A. & HERASIMCHUK, E. 1971, The multiple prediction of phonological variables in a bilingual speech community. In J. A. FISHMAN, R. COOPER & R. MA (eds), *Bilingualism in the Barrio*. 465–79.
FISHMAN, J. A. & HOFMAN, J. E. 1966, Mother Tongue and Nativity in the American Population. In J. A. FISHMAN (ed.), *Language Loyalty in the United States. The Maintenance and Perpetuation of Non-English Mother Tongues by American Ethnic and Religious Groups*. The Hague: Mouton. 34–50.
FRAENKEL, G. 1967, *Languages of the World*. Boston, Mass.: Ginn and Company.
FRIENDLY, M. L. & GLUCKSBERG, S. 1970, On the Description of Subcultural Lexicons: A Multidimensional Approach, *Journal of Personality and Social Psychology*, 14, 1, 55–65.
FRY, D. 1958, Experiments in the perception of stress. *Language and Speech*, 1, 126–52.
FU, G. B. S. 1975, *A Hong Kong Perspective: English Language Learning and the Chinese Student*. Unpublished Ph.D. thesis. University of Michigan.
— 1979, Bilingual Education in Hong Kong: a historical perspective. *Working Papers in Language and Language Teaching*, 1. Language Centre, University of Hong Kong: 1–19.
GARDNER, R. C. & TAYLOR, D. M. 1968, Ethnic stereotypes: their effects

on person perception. *Canadian Journal of Psychology*, 22, 4, 267–76.

GIBBONS, J. P. 1979a, Code Mixing and Koinéising in the Speech of Students at the University of Hong Kong. *Anthropological Linguistics*, 21, 3, 113–23.

— 1979b, U-gay-wa: a linguistic study of the campus language of students at the University of Hong Kong. In R. LORD (ed.), *Hong Kong Language Papers*. Hong Kong: Hong Kong University Press, 3–43.

— 1980, A tentative framework for speech act description of the utterance particle in conversational Cantonese. *Linguistics*, 18: 763–75.

— 1982, The Issue of the Language of Instruction in the Lower Forms of Hong Kong Secondary Schools. *Journal of Multilingual and Multicultural Development*, 3, 2, 117–28.

— 1983, *Code Choice and Code-Mixing in the Speech of Students at the University of Hong Kong*. Unpublished Ph.D. thesis. Reading: Department of Linguistic Science, University of Reading.

— 1984, Interpreting the English Proficiency Profile in Hong Kong, *RELC Journal* 15, 1, 46–74.

GIGLIOLI, P. P. (ed.) 1972, *Language and Social Context: Selected Readings*. Harmondsworth: Penguin.

GILES, H. (ed.) 1977, *Language, Ethnicity and Intergroup Relations*. London: Academic Press.

GILES, H. & BOURHIS, R. Y. 1976, Methodological Issues in Dialect Perception: Some Social Psychological Perspectives. *Anthropological Linguistics*, 18, 7, 294–304.

GILES, H., BOURHIS, R. Y. & TAYLOR, D. M. 1977, Towards a Theory of Language in Ethnic Group Relations. In H. Giles (ed.), *Language, Ethnicity and Intergroup Relations*. 307–48.

GILES, H. & POWESLAND, P. F. 1975, *Speech Style and Social Evaluation*. London: Academic Press.

GILES, H., ROBINSON, W. P. & SMITH, P. M. (eds) 1980, *Language Social Psychological Perspectives*. Oxford: Pergamon.

GILES, H. & SMITH, P. M. 1979, Accommodation Theory: Optimal Levels of Convergence. In H. GILES & R. ST CLAIR (eds), *Language and Social Psychology*. 45–65.

GILES, H., SMITH, P. M. & ROBINSON, W. P. 1980, Social Psychological Perspectives on Language: Prologue. In H. GILES, W. P. ROBINSON & P. M. SMITH (eds), *Language Social Psychological Perspectives*. 1–7.

GILES, H. & ST CLAIR, R. N. (eds) 1979, *Language and Social Psychology*. Oxford: Blackwell.

GIMSON, A. C. 1970, *An Introduction to the Pronunciation of English*. London: Arnold.

GOFFMAN, E. 1971, *The Presentation of Self in Everyday Life*. Harmondsworth: Penguin (first published 1959).

GUMPERZ, J. J. 1966, Linguistic Repertoires, Grammars, and Second
Language Instruction. *Monograph No. 18, Report of the Sixteenth
Annual Round Table Meeting on Linguistics and Language Study.*
Washington, D.C.: Georgetown University Press. 81–91. Also in J. J.
GUMPERZ *Language in Social Groups: essays by John J. Gumperz.*
177–89. (Page references are to this version)

— 1969, How Can We Describe and Measure the Behaviour of Bilingual
Groups. In L. G. KELLY (ed.), *Description and Measurement of
Bilingualism: An international seminar, University of Moncton, June
6–14, 1967.* 242–49.

— 1971, *Language in Social Groups: essays by John J. Gumperz*, selected
and introduced by A. A. Dil. Stanford: Stanford University Press.

— 1976, The sociolinguistic significance of conversational code-switching.
In J. COOK-GUMPERZ & J. J. GUMPERZ (eds), *Papers on language and
context*. Berkeley: University of California, Language Behaviour Research Laboratory. 1–46.

— 1982 *Discourse Strategies*. Cambridge: Cambridge University Press.

GUMPERZ, J. J. & HERNÁNDEZ-CHAVEZ, E. 1971, Bilingualism, Bidialectal-
ism, and Classroom Interaction. In J. J. GUMPERZ *Language in Social
Groups: essays by John J. Gumperz.* 311–39. Also in C. B. CAZDEN, V.
P. JOHN & D. HYMES (eds), *Functions of Language in the Classroom.*
New York: Teachers College Press. 84–108

GUMPERZ, J. J. & HYMES, D. (eds) 1972, *Directions in Sociolinguistics: the
ethnography of communication*. New York: Holt, Rinehart and Winston.

HALL, R. A., Jr. 1944, Chinese Pidgin English: grammar and texts.
Journal of the American Oriental Society, 64, 95–113.

— 1966, *Pidgin and Creole Languages*. Ithaca, New York: Cornell
University Press.

HELLER, M. (ed.) forthcoming, *Code-Switching*.

HSÜ, R. S. W. 1979, What is Standard Chinese?. In R. LORD (ed.), *Hong
Kong Language Papers*. Hong Kong: Hong Kong University Press.
115–41.

HUDSON, R. A. 1980, *Sociolinguistics*. Cambridge: Cambridge University
Press.

HUERTA, A. G. 1978, *Code Switching among Spanish-English Bilinguals: A
Sociolinguistic Perspective*. Unpublished Ph.D. dissertation. Austin:
University of Texas at Austin.

HUNTER, D. B. 1974, Bilingualism and Hong Kong English. *The Educa-
tionalist*. 5, 15–18.

HYMES, D. H. 1967, Models of the interaction of language and social setting. *Journal of Social Issues*, 23, 2, 8–28.

— 1968, The Ethnography of Speaking. In J. FISHMAN (ed.), *Readings in the Sociology of Language*. 99–138. First published in T. GLADWIN & W. STURTEVANT (eds) (1962) *Anthropology and Human Behaviour*. Washington, D.C.: Anthropological Society of America. 15–53.

HYMES, D. H. (ed.) 1971a, *Pidginization and Creolization of Languages*. London: Cambridge University Press.

— 1971b, Introduction. In D. HYMES (ed.), *Pidginization and Creolization of Languages*. 65–90.

— 1972, On Communicative Competence. In J. PRIDE & J. HOLMES (eds), *Sociolinguistics*. 264–93.

— 1977, *Foundations in Sociolinguistics. An Ethnographic Approach*. London: Tavistock.

I.P.A. INTERNATIONAL PHONETIC ASSOCIATION 1970, *The Principles of the International Phonetic Association*. London: International Phonetic Association.

JACKSON, J. 1974, Language Identity of the Colombian Vaupés Indians. In R. BAUMAN & J. SHERZER (eds), *Explorations in the Ethnography of Speaking*. 50–64.

JONES, D. 1967, (Revised by Gimson, A. C.) *Everyman's English Pronouncing Dictionary*. 13th Edition. London: J. M. Dent & Sons Ltd.

KACHRU, B. 1978, Towards Structuring Code-Mixing: an Indian Perspective. *International Journal of the Sociology of Language*, 16, 27–46.

KARTUNNEN, F. 1976, Finnish in America: A Case in Monogenerational Language Change. In B. BLOUNT & M. SANCHES (eds), *Sociocultural Dimensions of Language Change*. New York: Academic Press. 173–84.

KELLY, L. G. (ed.) 1969, *Description and Measurement of Bilingualism: an international seminar, University of Moncton, June 6–14, 1967*. Toronto: University of Toronto Press.

KRATOCHVÍL, P. 1970, *The Chinese Language Today: Features of an Emerging Standard*. London: Hutchinson.

KWOK, H., CHAN, M. & SUN, A. 1972, Where the Twain do Meet: a preliminary study of the language habits of university undergraduates in Hong Kong. *General Linguistics*, 12, 2, 63–82.

LABOV, W. 1966, *The Social Stratification of English in New York City*. Washington, D.C.: Center for Applied Linguistics.

— 1970, The Study of Language in its Social Context. *Studium Generale*, 23, 30–87. Reprinted in J. A. FISHMAN, *Advances in the Sociology of Langugage*, 1, 152–216. References are to this version. And in W. LABOV *Sociolinguistic Patterns*, 183–259.

— 1972, *Sociolinguistic Patterns*. Philadelphia: University of Pennsylvania Press. References are to Oxford: Blackwell (1978) version.

LAMBERT, W. E., FRANKEL, H. & TUCKER, G. R. 1966, Judging Personality Through Speech: A French–Canadian Example. *Journal of Communication*, 16, 4, 305–21.

LAMBERT, W. E., HODGSON, R. C., GARDNER, R. C. & FILLENBAUM, S. 1960, Evaluation reactions to spoken Languages. *Journal of Abnormal and Social Psychology*, 60, 1, 44–51.

LAVER, J. & TRUDGILL, P. 1979, Phonetic and Linguistic Markers in Speech. In K. R. SCHERER & H. GILES *Social Markers in Speech*. 1–32.

LEPAGE, R. B. 1978, Projection, focussing and diffusion, or steps towards a sociolinguistic theory of language, illustrated from the sociolinguistic survey of multilingual communities, stages I: Belize (British Honduras) and II: St. Lucia. Society for Caribbean Linguistics Occasional Paper 9, Mimeo. School of Education, University of the West Indies, St. Augustine, Trinidad. Reprinted in *York Papers in Linguistics*, 9.

LEPAGE, R. B. & TABOURET-KELLER, A. forthcoming, *Acts of Identity*.

LIEBERSON, S. 1969, How can we describe and measure the incidence and distribution of bilingualism? In L. G. KELLY (ed.), *Description and Measurement of Bilingualism: an international seminar, University of Moncton, June 6–14, 1967*. 286–95.

LINDESMITH, A. R. & STRAUSS, A. L. 1967, *Social Psychology*. New York: Holt, Rinehart and Winston.

LORD, R. (ed.) 1979, Hong Kong Language Papers. Hong Kong: Hong Kong University Press.

LUELSDORF, W. A. 1975, *A Segmental Phonology of Black English*. The Hague: Mouton.

LUKE, K. K. & RICHARDS, J. C. 1982, English in Hong Kong: functions and status. *English World-Wide: A Journal of Varieties of English*, 3, 1, 47–64.

LYCZAK, R., FU, G. S. & HO, A. 1976, Attitudes of H. K. Bilinguals toward English and Chinese Speakers. *Journal of Crosscultural Psychology*, 7, 4, 425–37. Also in R. LORD (ed.), *Hong Kong Language Papers*. 62–71. (Under title 'Language attitudes among University students in Hong Kong.')

MA, R. & HERASIMCHUK, E. 1971, The Linguistic Dimensions of a Bilingual Neighbourhood. In J. FISHMAN, R. COOPER, & R. MA (eds), *Bilingualism in the Barrio*. 347–464.

McCLURE, E. F. 1977, Aspects of Code-Switching in the Discourse of Bilingual Mexican-American Children. *Technical Report #44*. Urbana: Center for the Study of Reading, University of Illinois.

McCLURE, E. F. & WENTZ, J. 1975, Functions of Code Switching among

Mexican–American Children. In R. E. GROSSMAN, L. J. SAN & T. M. VANCE *Papers from the Parasession on Functionalism*. Chicago: Chicago Linguistic Society: 421–432.

MILROY, L. 1980, *Language and Social Networks*. Oxford: Blackwell.

NEWNHAM, R. 1971, *About Chinese*. Harmondsworth: Penguin.

NIDA, E. A. & FEHDERAU, H. W. (1970), Indigenous Pidgins and Koinés. *International Journal of American Linguistics*, 36, 2, 146–55.

OHANESSIAN, S., FERGUSON, C. A. & POLOMÉ, E. C. 1975, *Language Surveys in Developing Nations; papers and reports on sociolinguistic surveys*. Arlington, Virginia: Center for Applied Linguistics.

OSGOOD, C. E., MAY, W. H. & MIRON, M. S. 1975, *Cross Cultural Universals of Affective Meaning*. Urbana: University of Illinois Press.

OSGOOD, C. E., SUCI, G. J. & TANNENBAUM, P. H. 1957, *The Measurement of Meaning*. Urbana: University of Illinois Press.

PAN, P. G. 1982, Hong Kong Cantonese: A Sociolinguistic Perspective. *Working Papers in Linguistics and Language Teaching*, 6, 1–16. Language Centre, University of Hong Kong.

PARKIN, D. 1971, Language Choice in Two Kampala Housing Estates. In W. H. Whiteley (ed.), *Language Use and Social Change*. London: Oxford University Press. 347–63.

PARKIN, D. 1974, Language Switching in Nairobi. In W. H. WHITELEY (ed.), *Language in Kenya*. 189–216.

PASCASIO, E. M. (ed.) 1977, *The Filipino Bilingual: Studies on Philippine Bilingualism and Bilingual Education*. Quezon City: Ateneo de Manila University Press.

PFAFF, C. W. 1979, Constraints on Language Mixing: Intrasentential Code-Switching and Borrowing in Spanish/English. *Language*, 55, 2, 291–318.

PIERSON, H. D. & BOND, M. H. 1982. How do Chinese Bilinguals Respond to Variations of Interviewer Language and Ethnicity? *Journal of Language and Social Psychology*, 1, 2.

PIERSON, H. D., FU, G. S. & LEE, S. Y. 1980, An Analysis of the relationship between language attitudes and English attainment of secondary students in Hong Kong, *Language Learning*, 30, 289–316.

PLATT, J. T. 1975, The Singapore English Speech Continuum and its Basilect 'Singlish' as a 'Creoloid'. *Anthropological Linguistics*, 17, 7, 363–74.

— 1977, Code Selection in a Multilingual-Polyglossic Society. *Talanya*, 4, 64–75.

POPLACK, S. 1980, Sometimes I'll start a sentence in Spanish Y TERMINO EN ESPANOL: toward a typology of code-switching. *Linguistics*, 18, 581–618.

POSTIGLIONE, G. A. 1983, *Ethnicity and American Social Theory: toward Critical Pluralism*. Washington, D.C.: University Press of America.

PRIDE, J. B. & HOLMES, J. 1972, *Sociolinguistics*. Harmondsworth: Penguin.

QUIRK, R. & GREENBAUM, S. 1973, *A University Grammar of English*. London: Longman. (References are to English Language Book Society edition.)

RAYFIELD, J. R. 1970, *The Language of a Bilingual Community*. The Hague: Mouton.

ROSS, J. A. 1979, Language and the Mobilization of Ethnic Identity. In H. GILES & B. SAINT-JACQUES (eds), *Language and Ethnic Relations*. Pergamon: Oxford. 1–13.

RUBIN, J. 1968, *National Bilingualism in Paraguay*. The Hague: Mouton.

RUBIN, J. & JERNUDD, R. (eds) 1972, *Can Language be Planned? Sociolinguistic theory and practice for developing nations*. Honolulu: University of Hawaii Press.

RYAN, E. B. 1979, Why do Low-Prestige Varieties Persist? In H. GILES & R. ST CLAIR (eds), *Language and Social Psychology*. Oxford: Blackwell. 145–57.

RYAN, E. B. & CARRANZA, M. A. 1975, Evaluative Reactions of Adolescents towards Speakers of Standard English and Mexican American Accented English. *Journal of Personality and Social Psychology*, 31, 5, 855–63.

SANKOFF, D. (ed.) 1978, *Linguistic Variation: Models and Methods*. New York: Academic Press.

SANKOFF, D. & LABERGE, S. 1978, Successive Occurrences of a Variable in Discourse. In D. SANKOFF (ed.), *Linguistic Variation: Models and Methods*. 119–27.

SANKOFF, G. 1972, Language Use in Multilingual Societies: some Alternative Approaches. In J. B. PRIDE & J. HOLMES (eds), *Sociolinguistics*. Harmondsworth: Penguin. 31–51.

SANKOFF, G. & VINCENT, D. 1977, L'emploi productif du ne dans le francais parlé à Montréal. *Langue Française*, 34: 81–108.

SAVILLE-TROIKE, M. 1982, *The Ethnography of Communication: an Introduction*. Oxford: Blackwell.

SCHERER, K. R. & GILES, H. (eds) 1979, *Social Markers in Speech*. Paris and Cambridge: Editions de la Maison des Sciences de l'Homme and Cambridge University Press.

SCOTTON, C. M. 1976, Strategies of Neutrality: Language Choice in Uncertain Situations. *Language*, 52, 4, 919–41.

— 1980, Explaining Linguistic Choices as Identity Negotiations. In H. GILES, W. P. ROBINSON & P. M. SMITH (eds), *Language Social Psychological Perspectives*. 359–66.

— 1983, The Negotiation of Identities in Conversation: a Theory of Markedness and Code Choice. *International Journal of the Sociology of Language*, 44, 115–36.

SCOTTON, C. M. & URY, W. 1977, Bilingual strategies: the social functions of code-switching. *International Journal of the Sociology of Language*, 13, 5–20.

SETLUR, P. H. 1973, Towards a Theory of Code Switching. Unpublished M. A. Project. Lancaster: University of Lancaster.

SMITH, P. M. 1979, Sex Markers in Speech. In K. R. SCHERER & H. GILES (eds), *Social Markers in Speech*. 109–46.

SRIDHAR, S. N. 1978, On the Functions of Code-Mixing in Kannada, *International Journal of the Sociology of Language*, 16, 109–17.

THOMPSON, R. W. 1960, O Dialecto Português de Hong Kong. *Boletim de Filologia*, 19, 289–93.

TIMM, L. A. 1975, Spanish-English Code-Switching: El Porqué y How-Not-To. *Romance Philology*, 28, 4, 473–82.

TONGUE, R. & GIBBONS, J. P. 1982, Structural Syllabuses and the Young Beginner. *Applied Linguistics*, 3, 1, 60–69.

TRUDGILL, P. 1972, Sex, Covert Prestige and Linguistic Change in the Urban British English of Norwich. *Language in Society*, 1, 179–95.

— 1974, *The Social Differentiation of English in Norwich*. Cambridge: Cambridge University Press.

— (ed.) 1978, *Sociolinguistic Patterns in British English*. London: Arnold.

TRUDGILL, P. & TZAVARAS, G. A. 1977, Why Albanian–Greeks are not Albanians: Language Shift and Ethnicity in Attica and Biotia. In H. GILES (ed.), *Language, Ethnicity and Intergroup Relations*. London: Academic Press: 171–84.

TURNER, R. (ed.) 1974, *Ethnomethodology*. Harmondsworth: Penguin.

URE, J. 1974, Code switching and "mixed speech" in the register systems of developing languages. In A. VERDOODT (ed.), *Proceedings of the Third International Congress of Applied Linguistics*, II. Heidelberg: J. Groos Verlag.

WEINREICH, U. 1974, *Languages in Contact: findings and problems*. The Hague: Mouton. Originally published 1953. New York: Linguistic Circle of New York.

WELLS, G. (ed.) 1981, *Learning through interaction: the study of language development*. Cambridge: Cambridge University Press.

WENTZ, J. 1977, *Some considerations in the development of a syntactic description of code-switching*. Unpublished Ph.D. dissertation: University of Illinois at Urbana-Champaign.

WESTCOTT, K. 1977, *Survey of the Use of English in Hong Kong*. Hong Kong: unpublished mimeo.

WHINNOM, K. 1971, Linguistic Hybridization and the Special Case of Pidgins and Creoles. In D. HYMES (ed.), *Pidginization and Creolization of Languages*. London: Cambridge University Press. 91–115.

WHITELEY, W. H. (ed.) 1974, *Language in Kenya*. Nairobi: Oxford University Press.

WOLFRAM, W. A. 1969, *A Sociolinguistic Description of Detroit Negro Speech*. Washington, D.C.: Center for Applied Linguistics.

WRIGHT, A. F. (ed.) 1953, *Studies in Chinese Thought*. Chicago: University of Chicago Press.

YANG, K. S. & BOND, M. H. 1980, Ethnic Affirmation by Chinese Bilinguals. *Journal of Cross-Cultural Psychology*, 11, 4, 411–25.

Index

169